October 1977

Dear John,

On this occasion of your 25th Anniversary, I accompany with gladness and prayer. I thank you for your beautiful witness and example of the Gospel values of faith and faithfulness, love and service, being the poor man and oh so generous.

Your brother,
Tom Lemoncsc

FRANCIS OF ASSISI

Commemorating
the 750th anniversary
of the death of St. Francis,
1226 - 1976

FRANCIS OF ASSISI

An Essay by Walter Nigg,
with Extracts from the Lives
by Bonaventure, Thomas of Celano,
and the Three Companions

and
71 Color Photographs
by Toni Schneiders

Translated by William Neil

FRANCISCAN HERALD PRESS
1434 WEST 51st STREET • CHICAGO, 60609

Francis of Assisi, an Essay by Walter Nigg, with Extracts from the Lives by Bonaventure, Thomas of Celano, and the Three Companions, and 72 Color Photographs by Toni Schneiders, translated by William Neil from the German, *Der Mann von Assisi,* © copyright 1975 Verlag Herder KG Freiburg im Breisgau. English edition © copyright 1975 Franciscan Herald Press, 1434 West 51st Street, Chicago, Illinois 60609.

First published in 1975 by Franciscan Herald Press and A. R. Mowbray & Co., The Alden Press, Osney Mead, Oxford

Library of Congress Cataloging in Publication Data:

Main entry under title:

Francis of Assisi.

Translation of Der Mann von Assisi.
1. Francesco d'Assisi, Saint, 1182-1226.
I. Nigg, Walter, 1903-
BX4700.F6M3413   271′.3′024 [B]   75-25662
ISBN 0-8199-0586-0

NIHIL OBSTAT:
Mark Hegener O.F.M.
Censor

IMPRIMATUR·
Msgr. Richard A. Rosemeyer, J.D.
Vicar General, Archdiocese of Chicago

MADE IN THE UNITED STATES OF AMERICA

Contents

Foreword

By the Right Rev. John R. H. Moorman,
Bishop of Ripon

St. Francis of Assisi is one of the most popular of all the saints. Every year we are bombarded with books, pictures, statuettes, plays and films. The reasons for this are many. The first is that we know so much about him. As Walter Nigg says (p. 1), "there are few medieval personalities about whom we are so well informed as we are about St. Francis." Then again, his life is full of drama—the stages of his conversion, his renunciation before his father, his journey to the sultan of Egypt, his preaching to the birds, his dealings with the popes, and so on. Again, St. Francis stands for very simple ideals. Brother Leo once said that the four foundation-stones of their life were Poverty, Humility, Simplicity, and Prayer. There was nothing complicated or abstruse about the Franciscan way of life. Its originality lay in its intensity and imagination. Finally, St. Francis appeals to us because, unlike other men devoted to the religious life, he went about among the people. He wanted to help the helpless and love the unlovely and unlovable. He penetrated into the worst slums of the medieval cities in search of the sick and the poor. He lived among the outcasts and the lepers. This was a new kind of "religious" life, and it is one which appeals to us very strongly today.

All these things have made St. Francis a very popular and beloved saint. But if we are to understand him and appreciate the contribution which he has made to the Christian world we must look very carefully at what he said and what he did.

The basis of Francis' experiment in Christian living was total obedience to the recorded commands of Christ. No one can read the Gospels without an uneasy feeling that Jesus was, perhaps, asking too much. We read his "hard sayings" and begin at once to find good reasons for not accepting them. We don't sell all that we have and give to the poor. We don't go on journeys taking nothing with us. We don't turn the other cheek. We don't go "the second mile." In fact, we try to persuade ourselves that these orders were not meant for ordinary people like us. But Francis was not an ordinary person. He had no desire to look for an escape-route. All he wanted to do was to take Christ seriously — and face the consequences.

We must not, therefore, be misled by pictures of St. Francis in a clean and tidy habit, wandering about in a warm, sunlit, Italian landscape, accompanied by some of the more lovable wild creatures. We must remember that the first thing which happened to him when he had broken all links with the past by giving back to his father everything he had (including the clothes he was wearing) was to be thrown into a pit filled with snow and left there to die of exposure and frostbite. Soon after this we find him living among the lepers, eating and sleeping with them regardless of the filth and stench and the appalling risks which he ran.

So it was all through his life. Francis lived in a world of hunger, poverty, dirt, and disease. These were the things which he willingly endured in order to show that the teaching of Christ was not just an impossible ideal but a practical way of life for those who were prepared to take the consequences. This, inevitably, made him very careful about those whom he accepted as disciples. Just as Jesus refused to take men who were not prepared to follow him without question — (it was, after all, a reasonable excuse to say that you wanted to go to your father's funeral) — so St. Francis was very severe on those who, in any way, fell short of his ideal. A young man who wanted to join the party but who, instead of giving his property to the poor gave it to his relations, was sent packing. "Buzz off, Brother Fly" said the saint to him, "you're no good to us." And so it was all through his life. Francis could mete out very harsh punishments to those who failed to come up to his standards of poverty and humility.

Life was, indeed, very hard for St. Francis and those who went with him. Look at pictures 35 and 54 in this book and ask yourself what it would be like to have to sleep, without any sort of bedclothes, in such a place and not to know whether you would get anything to eat on the following day. "Poverty" and "Humility" — these are words which occur over and over again in the stories of St. Francis. As Nigg says (p. 8), "the Poverello wanted to be as poor as poor could be, and watched like a jealous lover to ensure that no one should rob him of his darling Poverty, which he experienced as a new kind of freedom. His passionate love of Poverty must not, however, be glamorized in any romantic way: it meant renunciation and deprivation, hunger and cold."

The Introduction to this book will help us to realize the total renunciation which Francis made and which he lived out for twenty arduous years. I hope it will encourage people to look again at the early accounts of the saint, some of them written by his own friends. Above all, I would recommend chapter 8 of *The Little Flowers of St. Francis*, which, better than anything else, expresses the Franciscan ideal. We need, from time to time, to do this if we are going to understand the true St. Francis in all his courage and self-discipline and see him as a living example of what St. Paul called "the goodness and the severity of God." It is then that we shall begin to understand why Francis has a very special message to us today in this affluent, complacent, selfish, materialistic society in which we live.

FRANCIS, THE LITTLE BROTHER FROM ASSISI

by Walter Nigg

The Secret of St. Francis

"No one can utter the name of St. Francis without experiencing a great sweetness," wrote Brother Giles, one of the earliest of the saint's companions. This unusual guideline points the way to St. Francis. We cannot get close to him through scholarship, criticisms, or science; for, all these methods are ruled out in advance and entirely fail to penetrate the secret of this man. Brother Giles's warning is doubly apt. Are we entitled to add another publication to the vast body of literature about St. Francis? Would it not be better to honor the Poverello in silence? We cannot brush these questions aside, especially since we are constantly aware of Brother Gile's admonition: "No one can utter the name of St. Francis without experiencing a great sweetness." The claim of "great sweetness" is not made on behalf of St. Francis by outsiders. The saint himself often spoke of the sweetness that filled and overwhelmed his heart. It is thus completely out of the question to write about him in a cold dispassionate manner. Without obvious warmth and enthusiasm, joy and happiness, we shall not be directly affected by St. Francis. Francis' companions spoke of great "sweetness," and meant by that nothing mawkish, insipid, or pious — expressions which are more suited to earlier, cheap pictures of the saints. "Sweetness" is only a word for that which is inexpressible about St. Francis. The sweet essence of the saint is hidden in a hard shell, which has to be broken open in order to discover the precious contents of his heart. It is almost unimaginable that there should ever have existed on earth anyone who so closely resembled Christ. St. Francis cannot be grasped by the exercise of pure reason, because he is beyond any kind of intellectualism. Yet we can clearly sense the indescribable glory that streams from his inmost being.

There are few mediaeval personalities about whom we are so well informed as we are about St. Francis. Several different accounts sketch an astonishingly lively picture of the saint. The men of his own time were already writing about him. Celano was one of them and we also have first-class eyewitness accounts in the "Mirror of Perfection" and the "Story of the Three Companions." Admittedly these traditions are couched in legendary form — for this suits the "sweetness" which Brother Giles demanded. Lives of the saints are distinct from secular biographies. They do not at all deserve the low opinion which is held of them at the present day.

To describe a saint "as he really was" is a modern demand which, looked at closely, amounts to the same thing as adopting the point of view of a secular biographer, whereby the special character of hagiography disappears. If we take away the legendary elements, we have not really grasped the essence of the saint but have simply robbed the holy man of his fragrance, his atmosphere, his sweetness. This results, like all demythologising, in reducing the holy man to a skeleton. Behind the old legend lies a historical event artistically described. The attempt to arrive at a new conception of St. Francis must look at the saint realistically and mystically at the same time. If this is not done his image becomes noticeably faded. The combination of these two opposite points of view conceals within itself tension and dissolution. The polarity of hard realism and legendary interpretation constitutes the new unscientific hagiography which we are passionately seeking and which we are still far from finding. The soil of Umbria and the supernatural flow into one another in the case of St. Francis. Without an awareness of this union the allegorical and the sacred disappear. To understand the Poverello we need a new alphabet, an investigation which expresses itself in pictures and which looks at the timeless symbolism as tangibly as possible.

Contemporary reporters also felt the difficulty of their assignment and pathetically expressed their helplessness: "I remember almost word for word the sermons of all other preachers, yet what Francis says I am not able to reproduce; for even although I remember his words, it is always as if it had been different words that I hear from his mouth." What else does this remarkable confession mean than that St. Francis is a secret that lies above and beyond all words. The Poverello is described in many ways yet none of them can pin him down to a fixed formula. Let us try to appraise the power of his radiant personality so that a little of his great sweetness comes through to us.

Wasted Youth

St. Francis came of a well-to-do family. To be the son of rich parents is difficult and is far from being a privilege. There is a danger for young men in their parents' wealth. Young Francis had plenty of money at his disposal and spent it frivolously and thoughtlessly. He became the leader of the Assisi youth. The young people organized drinking parties and nightly bawled their way through the streets. Like many young men Francis in his early years lived from day to day and hardly gave a thought to life's problems.

Despite his superficial way of life at that time he had one characteristic which is worth noting. His manifest extravagance shows no trace of meanness in his nature. Francis was generous: he gave presents right and left and never regretted what he had given away. One day in his father's cloth warehouse in a busy moment he brusquely sent a beggar about his business and suffered immediately such remorse of conscience that he resolved in future to turn down no plea for help. Open-handedness was second nature to him from his earliest days and he maintained it throughout his whole life.

According to Celano's "Life," Francis in his young days dissipated his energy and frittered away his time. Until he was twenty-five he gloried in ostentation and empty vanity. He spent his time in amusement and got up to all sorts of mischief. His was a lost youth, filled with emptiness, as must unfortunately be said of many young people who grow up without any guiding principles or sense of direction. Modern biographers have been at pains to characterize Francis' wasted youth as being not too bad. This toning down of the truth may be well meant, but this glossing over of the blots on Francis' character has contributed to the lack of credibility in the case of earlier lives of the saint. All such embellishment contradicts the truth. In fact, at that time Francis walked the streets of Babylon, wallowed in his sins, and wantonly stirred up trouble. If we are not to believe Celano at this point we have no reason to trust his later reports. But we must reflect that the average conventional type of man seldom achieves anything unusual: he remains trapped in his spiritual mediocrity, but sometimes great sinners become great saints.

Unexpectedly certain events confronted Francis which he could not readily evade. During the war between Assisi and Perugia Francis was taken prisoner. What must have been his thoughts when he found himself staring at the grey prison walls? We cannot tell. At all events on his release he was a sick man. His proud plans for knightly enterprises dissolved overnight into nothing. He recovered but slowly, which brought about a visible change in him. The noisy activities of his comrades seemed flat and empty. Restlessly he fought against a real torment of spirit. If the inward change remained concealed, people felt it through certain things that took place and knew that something was starting that does not happen every day. In the words of Dante, "a new life is beginning."

Beginning of a New Life

The change lasted a long time but progressively took clearer shape until at last his associates realized that Francis had become a different man. He himself experienced his inward tumult as "a change from bitterness to sweetness," felt that someone stronger than himself had taken hold of him and was amazed at his own new attitude.

At last the young man recovered complete health and wandered lost in his dreams in the charming surroundings of Assisi. He often asked himself longingly: "What gives my life a meaning?" Unexpectedly he met a leper. Francis had always had a powerful horror of this disease. He could hardly bring himself even to look at these people. Even now the sight of this apparition covered with sores revolted him. There was in addition an unpleasant smell which he wanted to run away from as fast as he could. But something impelled him to force himself to give the leper alms and to kiss him.

How this unexpected greeting came about Francis could not explain. The scene is extraordinarily realistic: Francis touches with his lips the hand of a leper without the slightest fear of contagion! The sight was anything but pleasant. Just because our aesthetic sense is offended we must regard this encounter with the leper as the first step in his new awakening. Instead of expressing our natural disgust we should rather remember St. Francis' later words: "God let me begin my penance in this way: when I was still living a sinful life, I found it very difficult even to look at a leper: but God himself led me to them and I began to care for them, and what had been hard for me became easy and made me happy." It was his first victory over his natural inclinations, and Francis ascribed it wholly to God and not to himself. Right away St. Francis began to visit the hospital which was normally shunned by everybody. Lepers played an important role in his life. It was through them that he found bitterness turning to sweetness. Francis used this expression frequently, meaning that at the beginning of his Christian life a wonderful thing had happened to him which could not be explained in words.

A second experience of no less importance came to him. Francis went in one day to the half ruined church of San Damiano to pray before the crucifix there. While he was deep in prayer, the figure on the Cross spoke to him: "Francis do you not see that my house is in ruins? Go and rebuild it." At these words Francis was seized with violent trembling. He was the man to whom the figure on the Cross has spoken. Was it imagination, a dream, or a vision? It was none of these. It was a direct order from Christ. Is it difficult to understand that this event must be transferred to the realm of poetry? Is it not much more remarkable that so many people in their lifetime look at Romanesque crosses, Celtic high crosses, or even hang golden crucifixes round their necks and experience absolutely nothing? Can one really look at the Cross without feeling that it is speaking to us? In the case of Francis it was different: the crucified Son of God himself had told him in a gentle voice what he had to do. In that very hour Francis knew he had been called and that he could only answer the voice by his actions. From that day onwards St. Francis lived in a mystical relationship to Christ, which in this conspicuous way had become an example.

Francis understood that the words from the Cross were to be taken literally: he believed that he must rebuild San Damiano. So he collected stones, mixed mortar, and rebuilt the little church. This was no mistaken task, for neglected churches are not pleasing to God. But it was a limited enterprise. His assignment was to be more far-reaching as the saint came in time to realize. He had to renew the whole Church in his day from its devitalized state and not merely to prop it up. Without setting himself up as a Reformer he became one of the great revivers of the Church and brought her back to her true vocation. This activity enlarged his significance, which extended far beyond that of the founder of an Order.

Wedded to Poverty

It was not long before Francis was invited to a feast by his former companions. He did not yet possess the inward resolution to say "No," and he sat among them although the raucous songs no longer meant anything to him. In the midst of the stupid uproar a deep sadness came upon him. He got quieter and finally fell silent altogether. His change in demeanor was observed and one of them said jokingly: "Francis is thinking of his girl friend." As his friends shouted with laughter Francis got up and, moved by some inexplicable impulse, said to his drinking companions: "Yes, he's right. I'm thinking of taking a wife. I'm going to marry Poverty." The words were out of his mouth before he realized their implications. He left the room amid a roar of laughter from his friends and never went back to them.

Francis' wedding with Poverty is beyond ordinary understanding, but it reveals the essence of his concern. Lady Poverty became for him a personalized figure, with whom he embarked on a marriage which was a real one and by no means merely symbolic. She was his bride, mother, and mistress at the same time. It was as much a physical bond as that between man and wife. If we cannot begin to grasp that Poverty was the one thought in his life we shall never come close to St. Francis. He embraced Poverty like a sweetheart and pressed her to his heart. Nothing else must come between God and himself. Poverty — an abbreviation for the penniless life of Christ — did not weigh as heavily on him as on other poor folk. He had become poor of his own free will and had thereby gained inward riches beyond compare. St. Francis spoke of "holy poverty," for whoever sees poverty sees Christ. Whereas the man who wants possessions thinks only of laying his hands on more and more things that he can call his own, never has enough, and always harbors new desires, Francis did the exact opposite: he got rid of all his possessions, threw them like rubbish out of the window, and wanted absolutely nothing more.

The Poverello wanted to be as poor as poor could be, and watched like a jealous lover to ensure that no one should rob him of his darling Poverty, which he experienced as a new kind of freedom. His passionate love of Poverty must however not be glamorized in any romantic way: it meant renunciation and deprivation, hunger and cold. St. Francis often lodged in caves and holes in the ground, where he sought shelter like some wild beast. For his acquaintances this life of poverty was an impossible undertaking which aroused either mockery or anger. He had to live the life of a beggar holding out his bowl at people's doors for them to throw him scraps of any kind. Eventually his appearance was almost revolting. The Poverello with his disciples wanted to embody the poverty of the life of Christ who said: "Foxes have holes and birds of the air have nests; but the Son of man has nowhere to lay his head." This involved frightful hardship from which any normal man would recoil. To carry it through to the end and get rid of everything could only succeed with a man who was wholly committed to Christ. Francis' idea of poverty cannot be traced back to the mediaeval attitude toward life. On the contrary, the Italian middle class was at that time on the threshold of an upsurge: the first signs of the intoxicating and gorgeous age of the early Renaissance were already apparent. Francis went the opposite way, he went down into the depths until he disappeared from human view. His marriage with Poverty, like the speaking crucifix, can only be understood from his mystical background. This mystical understanding, however, makes nonsense of any rational considerations. St. Francis who had become equal with the poor said: "Whoever reviles a beggar offends Christ, whose noble insignia every poor man wears; for it was for our sakes that Christ made himself poor in this world."

If we try to explain the significant but wholly unfashionable poverty of Francis, it is probably best expressed in the words of George Bernanos. The comments of the French poet are to be understood as asides which he has put into the mouth of St. Francis: "The outlook is bad, dear children, very bad — the saint would have said — and worse is yet to befall you. I wish I could comfort you about your state of health. But if herb teas would be enough for you I would happily have stayed at home, for I loved my friends dearly, I used to sing them provençal songs on the lute. Happiness is within your grasp. Do not try to reach it by devious ways — there is only one way, poverty. I shall not follow you along this road, little ones, I shall go ahead of you: I shall throw myself in front, have no fear! If I could suffer for myself alone, believe me, I should not have taken you away from your pleasures! But the good Lord has not allowed me to do this. You have insulted Poverty! What shall I say, you have driven her to the limit. Because she is patient you have little by little cunningly laid all your burdens on her shoulders. Now she lies stricken on the ground, without a word of complaint, her tears streaming into the soil. You say, trouble us no more now, now we can dance. But you will not dance, little ones, you will die. When Poverty curses you, you are dead. Don't bring the curse of Poverty on this world! Forward!" This contemporary speech of St. Francis sounds like the crack of a whip, corresponding to the temperamental poet, who intuitively understood the saint. Bernanos' fictitious speech of St. Francis shows us the way to the Poverello: only through a yearning for a new poverty can we get close to the saint and perhaps discover his true countenance.

A final experience brought St. Francis face to face with his ultimate goal. He attended Mass and heard Jesus' commission to his disciples: "Take no gold nor silver, nor copper in your belts, no bag for your journey, nor two tunics, nor sandals, nor a staff. . . ." At the end of the service Francis went to see the priest, asked him to read again the passage from Scripture and then clapped his hands with unspeakable joy. "That is what I want, that is what I am looking for, that is what I will do with all my heart." In that moment all his perplexity vanished. He knew from now on what precisely he wanted to do, and for him there was to be no more vacillation. The words of the Gospel had clinched the matter. Filled with overwhelming happiness he longed with his whole heart for nothing other than to follow the word of the Lord and to embody and revivify it in his own life.

The Break with His Father

One of the most exciting incidents in the life of St. Francis was the scene with his father. Wealthy and successful business man as he was, he could not possibly be in agreement with what he felt to be the fantastic ideas of his son. His own son had become the laughing stock of the town. Wounded in his honor, the father one day in a furious rage dragged his son across the town square into his house and locked him in a dark room. During the father's absence Francis' more gentle mother set him free. The father was at his wits' end and finally brought his son before the bishop, which led to an exciting legal tussle. In anticipation of the bishop's verdict many of the curious citizens were attracted into the market place. As the angry father accused his ungrateful son, who had, after all, his father to thank for all he had, Francis suddenly stripped off his clothes, stood naked in front of the crowd, and gave his robe back to his father with the words: "Listen all of you and pay heed: until now I have called Pietro Bernardone my father, but since I now propose to serve the Lord, I am giving him his money back which he is so concerned about, as well as all the clothes that he has paid for — from now on I shall say: 'Our Father who art in Heaven.'"

It was an unforgettable scene. Obviously Francis at that moment had no thought of the commandment: "Honor your father and your mother, that your days may be long in the land which the Lord your God gives you," a word from the Bible which is equally valid under the New Covenant. A higher obligation had prompted him to make the break with his father so decisive that it could not possibly be misunderstood. This extraordinary step shows that, according to Jesus' words, religious conversion separates a man from his family It cuts him off from his own flesh and blood and brings about a deep and lasting sorrow: this separation pierces his heart like a sword. It is not right to gloss over this renunciation of a father, nor can it be commended to young people for imitation. It makes a mockery of the love of a child for his parents. Francis' violent break with his father has hardly a parallel in the history of the saints. The Poverello himself found this alienation from his father thoroughly difficult, and he went through with it only under divine pressure. When he was later asked what had been the most difficult moment in his life, he merely whispered: "The affair with my father."

In the eyes of his contemporaries Francis after the breach with his father became a thirteenth-century layabout. He went about in clothes spattered with plaster and had a wild look about him. People peered at him over their shoulders, thought he had gone off his head, and children pelted him with mud. This is how Francis really looked to his contemporaries if we do not try to fit him into a saintly mould in advance. People in those days often shook their heads over him and played practical jokes on him. Even many of the priests were scandalized since they did not know what to make of him. Who can bear this reality? The question troubles our conscience.

Was Francis a Mediaeval Layabout?

Francis' rejection of the conventional society of his time seems to be a parallel to the revolt of young people at the present day against the older generation. The drop-outs of today want to claim him for themselves and think they are entitled to say: "Look at St. Francis, he was one of us! Why are you so concerned about our appearance?"

Is this claim justified? Was Francis really a mediaeval drop-out, or is this description lacking in respect? Superficially the comparison is understandable, but at one point there is a profound difference between Francis and the drop-outs which must not be overlooked.

Young people today let their hair grow long and run around in tattered clothes. They are protesting against a society that has become meaningless, that constantly takes on more and more soulless forms. In helpless anger they storm against a technological world in which they are at best mere ciphers. In their rage they would fain shatter this materialistic industrial society, but as to what to put in its place they have not the slightest conception. They are filled with confused ideas, picked up from anywhere, which they have never seriously thought through. The youth of today are completely at sea, as are their parents, who look at their children with alarm and anxiety. The spiritual need of our young people is great, for they are all looking for a new home and have no idea where to find it. So many of them take to drugs and face a horrible end, like the Children's Crusade in the Middle Ages which perished in darkness and terror.

Francis, however, knew what he wanted, and knew it so precisely that no one could lead him astray. At least he was never in any doubt after the crucifix had spoken to him and he had heard the words of Christ's commission. From then on Francis no longer drifted around aimlessly in the Assisi countryside: his apparent lack of purpose had taken quite a different turn. Everything had radically changed since Francis had now a new task to fulfil, compared with which everything else seemed trivial and futile. We need an objective, a clear solid objective. We need also to know the way to reach this objective, and must also feel that we are strong enough to get there if we are to measure up to our assignment. No one has ever yet accomplished anything with vague ideas and uncertain emotions. A serious study of the Poverello could help young people to reflect. They would have no need then to rush off to India chasing some mirage and ending up in misery. The timeless example is right in front of them ready to be translated into the modern idiom. Obviously this needs great determination, for to choose the way of St. Francis is no easy matter, not even in his own day and certainly not in ours. It means taking risks. Even coming to terms with him is not simple but involves an adventure which is a matter of life and death. But does this hazard not correspond to the deepest longings of young people in all ages?

The Imitation of Christ

Reviewing his various experiences Francis valued most the fact that he had been "instructed by God himself" and not by men as to which road he must take through life. "No one told me what I must do but Almighty God himself revealed to me that I must live in accordance with the holy gospel," wrote Francis in his Testament. According to this important pronouncement no person and no institution helped him to find the way. Neither mediator nor go-between came to his rescue in his perplexity. Francis underlined his direct instruction from God with the words: "He himself, Almighty God, revealed it to me." This immediate communication seemed incomprehensible to others, because they were unable to grasp it out of their own paltry experiences, and had no idea of what was really going on. The power of Christ had broken through in Francis: a burning passion was kindled within him. The picture of Christ which had been slowly receding arose afresh in his heart.

According to the testimony of the Poverello the Eternal himself had ordered him to live in accordance with the instructions of the holy gospel. In fact St. Francis can only be understood in connection with one saying from the gospel: "Follow me!" The word spoken by Christ to Matthew is the central command to which the whole life of St. Francis was subject. If we understand the gospel and consequent discipleship as unconditional, it leads to something close to self-identification. St. Francis used the expression "imitation of Christ" in no rhetorical way, nor was he enraptured with him. He accepted the command to become a disciple in utter seriousness, as seriously as probably no other Christian before or after him. He subordinated everything to this word of Christ; it lived in his soul, and he followed Christ so completely that it simply took conventional Christians' breath away.

The average citizen has his own ideas about what is meant by the imitation of Christ: "This is exaggerated, this is out of proportion, and that goes too far." It always goes too far for their comfort when the fire begins to burn of which Christ said: "I came to cast fire upon the earth; and would that it were already kindled." The life of St. Francis is nothing other than the perfect imitation of Christ. With all his strength and all his soul he devoted himself to it so that the whole undertaking reached extraordinary proportions and for us Christians quite unknown dimensions were opened up. That alone is the first service that Francis rendered to Christianity: he rescued it from its paralysis and placed it in a bold unusual situation, in which he steered without any security towards the absolute, which demanded men's supreme efforts.

St. Francis' discipleship is unique in the history of Christianity. It has a two-sided development, not in the sense of a hairsplitting dialectic which cancels the main proposition with a subordinate proposition. That would correspond to an intellectual game. To come to terms with the profundity of St. Francis even in small measure, we must take the two sides together. His imitation of Christ took place between two opposite poles which never sprang asunder under any strain. Francis contained this polarization within himself, to whom God had expressly given the order to be a new kind of fool in the world. Francis has made many easy-going Christians feel uncomfortable. The harsh and almost repellent Poverello must be seen in all his severity. Whoever has not recoiled from him in horror has not seen Francis of Assisi as he really was. It is not true that Francis was gentle and submissive. That is a misunderstanding of his character. He could be frightfully hard, not only in his personal asceticism but also in his relations with other people. "Just before his death he confessed that he had sinned greatly against 'brother ass,' meaning his body." He was capable of punishing the brothers severely if they did not carry out his orders. The closer one comes to the saint the more clearly one recognizes the sternness of his countenance. Various aesthetic books on St. Francis hide this inexorable side of him by depicting a charming landscape in which young friars play around with doves. This falsifies the true picture of St. Francis and distorts it into something aesthetic which one can unreservedly admire but which makes no demands on us. Aesthetic charm is deceptive. St. Francis himself would have consciously rejected it, even if without his approval it has had an effect on Giotto and other painters.

We must constantly set over against this supposedly charming Francis the true character of the Poverello, who followed the "naked Christ in his own nakedness" and was thus for his brothers "another Christ." To be a second Christ for the world is a noble, indeed unsurpassable title. Of course, the expression "another Christ" can easily be misunderstood. Many spiritually minded people have gone into raptures as they linked the figure of St. Francis with Joachim of Fiore's prophecy of the age of the Holy Spirit.

St. Francis himself remained sensible. Yet his inflexible imitation of Christ took on a form of likeness which reached the bounds of possibility.

St. Francis is the living symbol of Christ and the most intensive reminder of Christ. Christendom can never turn its back on either of these however much it may wilt and wither. When the world threatened to become frigid the hour of this saint of love had come. He deserves the title "the converter of the world."

The Little Brothers

It was not long before there were the makings of a brotherhood. Francis himself expressed it more modestly: "God gave me brothers."

The first to attach himself to him was Bernardo di Quintavalle. He was a rich man who sold all his property, gave the proceeds to the poor, and thenceforward shared his life with Francis. This companion was soon followed by a second and a third, so that the company steadily grew.

The brothers were faced with many problems. They were not sure whether they should live in the community among others or whether they should betake themselves to solitude. Francis knew that he had been sent to win souls for God and to renew the spiritual life of Christendom. As the brothers were distinct from the rest of the community in dress and way of life, they gave the impression of being "a kind of forest folk." They were also called "the Penitents from Assisi." St. Francis himself wanted to call them the "Order of Little Brothers," because they wished to be insignificant and to have no illusions of grandeur. The title "Little Brothers" goes back to St. Francis himself, who once said to his companions: "Take heart and rejoice in the Lord, and don't be downcast because there are so few of us! And don't let your simplicity and my own frighten you: God will make us into a very large brotherhood extending to the ends of the earth." People looked at them in astonishment as if they had come from another century. Francis gave the brothers a clear goal to attain. He wanted them to be shinging examples of the good life in the darkness of the world. The Poverello felt himself surrounded by sweet fragrance whenever he heard of the mighty works of the holy brothers who had gone out into the world. The Franciscan brotherhood was striving after a new way of life. That was its original concern. Francis was not interested in organization, theology, or scholarship. He saw his mission as embodying the gospel way of life. Everything else was secondary. The Franciscan way of life was the only thing that counted in the Poverello's eyes.

St. Francis demanded of his brothers that they should incarnate the poverty of Christ's life. The idea of poverty included a deliberate rejection of money. There was always a demonic element in money. It was Mammon, against God; and according to Jesus' words, a man cannot serve both at the same time. Francis wanted to be free of money, and tried to break its power through a new way of life. "He despised money so much that he thought of it as little as he did of dust." The rejection of money was no mere whim, for Francis knew the decision point at which many Christians meet their downfall. Money is a crossroads: either the Christian breaks through the money barrier or else he becomes its victim. Francis regarded money as trash: money and garbage were for him synonymous. The Poverello scolded a brother severely for simply touching money, and laid a hard penance on him.

Likewise Francis renounced all possessions for himself and his brothers. He wanted to possess neither houses nor monasteries; he wanted to live with his brothers like pilgrims in a foreign land and to prove it by his actions. Even the friendly bishop of Assisi could not understand his attitude. Francis' reply was: "My Lord, if we have possessions we must have weapons to defend ourselves. Hence come quarrels and battles which so often thwart the love of God and of our neighbors. Therefore we wish to own nothing temporal in this world." This astonishing utterance betrays an unsurpassable accuracy of aim. A simple man with a shrewd mind saw through a problem that many intellectuals inside and outside the Church do not want to tackle. St. Francis recognized the connection between Money — Property — Weapons — War, and drew the necessary conclusions. Christendom will never approach the abolition of wars until it thinks through these problems from the Franciscan point of view.

But since men have to live, St. Francis, while rejecting money, instructed the brothers to beg. In the present day we think of begging as something degrading: the modern state is eager to abolish beggars altogether. For Francis begging was an act of humility; he was the beggar *in excelsis*. Later on, and in the present day, young Franciscans regard begging as an alternative to working. But for Francis begging and working were not contradictory. His brothers often earned their keep by the labor of their hands, helping the peasants with the harvest. The Franciscan is no loafer, but he is not afraid to beg for alms when he possesses nothing himself, in order to cultivate humility in himself and to give his neighbors the opportunity to prove their generosity.

It is highly impressive to study the actions of the earliest brothers. There was no organization, it was all a matter of living. Unable to discuss the orders they had been given, they threw themselves into carrying them out, says Celano in his biography. No one thought of obedience as a burdensome affair which would be better replaced by the right to question and discuss, but rather thought of it as a great virtue: "I know the value of obedience, in that I submit to another with great profit to myself." To obey without question demands great self-subordination, which is genuinely Franciscan.

One can read in the record of those who lived with Francis what the life of the earliest brothers was like. A marvellous fragrance surrounds the occasion when Francis and the brothers celebrated Christmas in Greccio, a crib set up in the middle of the forest, so that they could after a fashion see the infant Jesus and experience a new Bethlehem. The brothers could not do as they liked. When the Emperor Otto IV passed through the region Francis forbade the brothers to view the procession. One brother alone was to approach the Emperor and say to him forcibly that his glory would last but a short time. His prophecy was proved right.

Francis himself hinted at the secret of the first brotherhood: "Let us begin, brothers, to serve the Lord, for so far we have made little progress." It was a command to make new beginnings constantly and never to sit back and rest contentedly when something had been achieved. Hence came the indescribable lustre which shines over the first period of the Franciscan movement.

The brotherhood grew apace, whereupon Francis devised a Rule for them. In this he fell back on neither the Rule of St. Benedict nor of St. Augustine as a pattern, for these had other aims in view. In all probability the first Rule, which has disappeared, consisted of a series of Biblical injunctions. St. Francis had no need of anything more. In time more precise instructions were needed, and eventually a second and a third Rule were devised. Francis found this difficult. That was understandable, for a true Christian way of life can never be fully regimented.

Nevertheless a community cannot exist without a Rule, otherwise it would easily run the risk of disintegrating. Even in the early days the Rule was resented. It was felt to be too severe and not all the brothers could live up to it. Francis, however, would not alter the words of Christ and once said gruffly: "Anyone who will not keep the Rule must leave the Order." In the last resort Francis himself was the Rule: to live in accordance with the gospel must be obligatory for all the brothers.

Eventually a Second Order was created, to include women members, the Poor Clares. The Third Order was intended for those who were to embody the ideal of Franciscan spirituality in the outside world. The idea of this Third Order came from St. Francis himself who clearly understood that not everybody could leave his home and his job. He also warned his brothers: "You must judge no man, or tolerate scornful criticism of those who live in luxury and dress in extravagant attire."

It is not possible in this essay to relate the history of the Order. That would need another book. According to Gemelli "the history of the Franciscan Order is an endless poem, to which every century has added its own verses." Like all history it flowed in waves, heights alternating with depths, while in between came recurring periods of stagnation.

During the lifetime of St. Francis the Portuguese Anthony of Padua was particularly renowned. The Poverello respected his vast learning, for he was at the same time a powerful preacher. Many legends were told of Anthony which helped to make him one of the most popular saints even to the present day. Another contemporary of St.

Francis was Elizabeth of Thuringia. She heard from one of the first of the Little Brothers in Germany about the Poverello's imitation of Christ, and with womanly intuition grasped his purpose. The great lady renounced her princely rights and devoted herself to the poor, and so she can be called the first tertiary in Germany.

Soon after St. Francis' death the fervor of the other-worldly members of the Order shook it to its foundations with their often reckless zeal. Amid these agitated disputations Bonaventure, who was as learned as he was humble, succeeded through his moderating influence in composing the opposing factions within the Order. Bonaventure was a saint: without his self-possession he would never have been able to bring about the urgently necessary pacification of the Order. He also wrote at the request of the General Chapter the officially recognized biography of St. Francis, which fixed his image for future generations for centuries.

The Franciscan Order has always produced great personalities, of whom only a few names can be mentioned. Alexander of Hales, Duns Scotus, Roger Bacon, Raymond Lull, and Berthold of Regensburg. The Franciscan community has proved to be an inexhaustible fountain. In the course of the centuries the Order has gained numerous historical honors, for which it also deserves recognition.

St. Francis and the Church

St. Francis intended to proclaim the glad tidings to the people through his brothers, as Christ had commanded in his missionary address to his disciples. Francis was not a great preacher, as the word is commonly understood. It transpired that words failed this formerly simple man and that he was no use as a speaker. He usually spoke in a powerful, understandable, pictorial style, corresponding to Biblical parables, because it seemed to him that inward power was more effective than all outward speech. The fire of his enthusiasm led him on one occasion, while he was speaking, to move his feet as if in a dance. He constantly relied on the inner compulsion of the Holy Spirit, and never adopted the style of a preacher but conveyed his thoughts in the form of conversation. In his public utterances he showed manly courage and love of the truth and was never afraid to call people's sins by their proper name without sparing anyone. Although he did not prepare his sermons carefully "he knew how to speak wonderfully well."

Francis and his first disciples were laymen, who could not automatically exercise a preaching office; they had therefore to get the permission of the Church. He therefore set out for Rome with his brothers, to seek permission from the Holy See. At that time Innocent III occupied the papal throne — one of the most powerful men to wear the tiara, but at the same time a man with an acute mind, wide legal training, and an imposing appearance. Innocent III recognized the need of the Church in his day, which troubled him even in his dreams. In a dream he saw the Church collapsing and saw also that it was propped up by one man — Francis certainly had the task of rebuilding a ruined church, which was not the same thing.

Francis humbly approached the powerful pope — it was a breathtaking moment in Church history. Time seemed to stand still. At first Innocent was disappointed by the unimpressive appearance of Francis, but he nevertheless engaged him in conversation. The majestic pope and the homely disciple of Christ embarked on a spiritual duel, and it remains a mystery how Francis in the power of his holy simplicity outplayed, overcame, and finally checkmated the clever pope, purely and simply by his incredible humility. It was only possible out of the inmost essence of the gospel. The pope did not give him documentary authorization — that came later from the successor of Innocent III — but he gave him verbally permission to preach, an assurance that sufficed Francis for the time being.

During a later visit to Rome Francis unexpectedly met St. Dominic, who was likewise seeking approval for his Order. This memorable meeting of the founders of the two mendicant Orders is surrounded by a mass of legends. But it is not merely legendary, it actually took place. Celano describes it fairly fully in his second biography. What the two men said to each other is not known in any detail: we are simply told that they had "agreeable intermittent conversations about the Lord." The cardinal then took part in the discussions and expressed the wish that in future bishops and other dignitaries should be chosen from the two Orders, because he would then get men who would light the way ahead for Christians by their teaching and example. Dominic and Francis were horrified at the bishop's proposal and decisively but politely declined it. In the opinion of the Poverello, his brothers "must always take the lowest place."

Francis saw Dominic as one of the most important men of his time. The Spaniard was a reserved but methodical man, who obliterated the traces of his life behind him, so that no garland of legends blossomed around his person as was the case with the Poverello. More than ten years older than Francis, he had travelled in many countries, and was consumed by a similar fervent love, as this saying indicates: "How can you browse over dead parchment while your brothers are dying of hunger!" In his rejection of ecclesiastical pomp and in his love of poverty he stood very close to St. Francis. In the encounter with the Poverello already referred to Dominic said: "I wish, Brother Francis, that your Order and mine could be united and that we could practise the same way of life within the Church." Dominic's proposal was certainly meant in earnest, yet Francis felt unable to accept it. However much their aims coincided, their approach was different, and the Poverello instinctively recognized this.

Dominic longed to collect priests round him, who certainly lived in poverty, but who were enabled through their studies to teach heretics in their sermons the error of their ways, whereas Francis was a layman and summoned his brothers to stir up an indifferent Christendom through a true imitation of Christ.

The two men who had spiritually so much in common took a touching farewell of each other (illustration 32). Dominic's last request to Francis was to present him with the rope which he used as a girdle. At first Francis refused, for he saw this as treating him with a reverence which was foreign to him. At length he gave in. Francis and Dominic grasped each other by the hand and took their leave with the utmost cordiality. Their fraternal embrace is for all Franciscans and Dominicans a constant reminder of their mutual friendship, which must not be tarnished by any ambitious rivalry.

Opposition between Francis and the Church was detected. It was said that Francis had changed his role and that Rome had conquered Assisi. That is an untenable position. Francis was in every respect a true son of the Church. He certainly wanted to be nothing else. It is possible that he at one time spoke reluctantly about the "pride of prelates," and about "their bad example which was a disgrace to the whole Church." He thought he could change the princes of the Church not by criticism but by holy humility and reverence. In principle he wanted "to keep the peace with the clergy." "Cover up their mistakes and try to make up for their many failures," was his admonition. Francis knew he had a mission to help the clergy, and the brothers went to the rescue when the clergy failed. He saw himself as "assistant to the priests" and deliberately refrained from any kind of polemic against the representatives of the Church. Even the cardinals realized this. Although they were clearly of the opinion that Francis' enterprise was "something within the Church that had never happened before," they did not dare to question his efforts, knowing full well that they would be renouncing the gospel.

Francis saw the faults of the mediaeval Church only too clearly. He certainly saw the incompatibility of clerical pomp with the penniless life of Christ ten times more acutely than critics of the Church then and now put together, nevertheless he would have nothing to do with protests and demonstrations. Cheap gestures of this kind cost nothing and spring mostly from self-importance. The Church can only be reformed by suffering for it. According to Francis a man only knows as much as he has made a reality.

He suffered for the Church with its abuses, suffered silently and painfully: because of this Christendom can never forget him. His image will accompany it through all time, for he has helped more than can be put into words. The saint adopted no anti-Christian, barren attitude, but bore the Church's frailties with the quiet acceptance of suffering, and that alone corresponds to the gospel way of life.

Brother Ever-glad

Francis was addressed by his brothers as "Brother Ever-glad." Despite his radical imitation of the penniless life of Christ the saint had nothing gloomy about him. He rebuked the brothers when they showed any signs of melancholy and used to say: "That is the Devil's greatest victory when he can rob any of God's servants of their joyful spirits." He regarded sadness as unseemly in a Christian. A brilliant radiance shone from his eyes which drew men to him as if by magic.

Cimabue was able to portray the inner joy of St. Francis with such artistic skill that it has become one of the most beautiful pictures of the saints of all times (illustration 39). The Poverello looks out of this icon at the beholder in a human, intimate, and friendly manner and awakes in him a boundless trust. An incomparable joy filled St. Francis. He was joy personified and loved to laugh and make fun, loved to sing his provençal songs, and possessed the kind of God-given humor that triumphed over all life's difficulties. He was never discouraged in any situation. Nothing was more foreign to him than pessimism and resignation. Joy, jubilant joy, was always victorious, and if ever a man on this solid earth has really understood the song of the angels on the plains of Bethlehem: "Behold we bring you good news of great joy which will come to all the people" it was the inimitable St. Francis. Joyfulness permeated every fibre of his being. It is almost incomprehensible how such a radiant joy should have streamed from him and how he attracted people to himself whether they wanted it or not. In St. Francis' own words: "What are the servants of God but his minstrels who move men's hearts and fill them with the gladness of the Spirit."

It is impossible to speak of all these things without experiencing the sweetness of which Brother Giles has spoken. It can almost be felt physically rippling through one's veins, when one is really gripped by the Poverello. The same inward inspiration was found among the Baal-worshippers, which is why the Franciscan movement and the Hasidim exhibit so many related characteristics.

This Christian joy was no mere human disposition in the case of St. Francis as he made his way around Umbria, it was rather a gift from heaven, because he had made himself fully open to the gospel. Only a man who has trodden the path of poverty right to the end can experience this kind of exhilarating joy. Everyone else must be content with a little sunshine, and never experience what the gospel calls joy, which alone satisfies men's deepest desires. Would not this joy be the cure for our joyless age, in which people eagerly chase after the smallest shred of pleasure, which always turns out to be a stale substitute?

St. Francis has himself given us a clear picture of what he meant by joy. His thoughts on perfect joy are to be found in the "Fioretti." The "Little Flowers of St. Francis" has been by-passed by historical research, since it first appeared in the fourteenth century. It is presupposed by research workers that the oldest sources are always the most reliable and that the youngest are questionable. Often, however, the oldest traditions are silent on very important matters for obvious reasons. At all events the "Little Flowers" are full of a genuine Franciscan spirit even if they are dependent on the working over of old records. They contain a chapter on joy in which that silent music can be heard which is generally shut off from human ears.

The story goes that Francis and Brother Leo were making their way from Perugia to St. Mary of the Angels. As they walked, Francis said repeatedly what perfect joy did *not* consist of, until at last Brother Leo said impatiently and completely at a loss: "Father, in God's name please tell me where perfect joy *is* to be found." St. Francis replied: "If we were soaked with rain and frozen with cold, filthy with mud off the roads and starving with hunger, and came to St. Mary of the Angels; and if we then rang the bell and the porter came out and said: "Who are you?" and if he then upon our replying: "We are your brothers" went on to say: "What? You are a couple of tramps wandering round extorting alms from the poor"; and if he would not open the door for us but left us standing well into the night in snow and water, frozen and hungry — and if we were to bear patiently all this hardship and these insults, quietly and without complaining, and if we were to think humbly and lovingly, this porter really knows us and God will have put these words into his mouth — there Brother Leo lies perfect joy."

The Message of Peace

It was out of his joy that there came also his message of peace. Francis bade the brothers greet people with the words: "May the Lord give you peace." The word "peace" lies likewise at the heart of the gospel: the angels sang at the birth of Christ of "peace on earth." The peace of the gospel is a gift from heaven and not of man's making — hence it cannot be created politically. Even pacifists despite their noble efforts cannot bring about the "Pax Christi," for peace comes from God. St. Francis possessed this peace. He embodied it in himself, and thus was able to reconcile quarrels between the cities of Italy by his mere presence. He spread around him an atmosphere of peace, for all that he did and said breathed peace. It was not only a postulated or desirable peace, it was something in the present, and had so to speak taken on a tangible bodily form, so that he literally poured out peace, a directly mystical happening, which cannot be rationally explained.

The most impressive example of peace was given by St. Francis in connection with his journey to the Holy Land, on which he embarked to undergo martyrdom. The century in which he lived was anything but ready for peace; weapons played a leading role, and people resorted to them at every opportunity. The Crusades moved and excited men's minds, and Francis himself was not against the idea — at least we are not told so — but he understood the Crusades more as a spiritual mission. At all events, he went to Palestine, not indeed like the other crusaders with a sword in his hand, but as a completely defenseless man, and thus set an incomparable example. Courageously he took the Christian crusaders to task for their dissolute behavior and foretold their defeat. The Poverello strode through the enemy lines, and although the soldiers made fun of him, they passed on his requests to the Sultan. Francis got his wish. He was taken into the Sultan's presence and spoke with his characteristic enthusiasm of the gospel. The Sultan listened to him and was impressed by his words. Clearly he felt that in Francis a powerful spirit was at work, one which was different from that of the crusaders. Although Francis was unable to change the military situation, or to settle it, he still made a powerful witness for peace. He could do this because the strength of Christ dwelt in him, an observation which brings us close to the secret of his personality.

Canticle of the Sun

Finally reference must be made to St. Francis' relationship to the created world. This inspired man looked at creation with open eyes and took into his heart all that crawls and flies, whatever has feelings and even whatever has no feelings. Francis preached to the birds as if they were rational beings. According to the legend they listened attentively and he made the sign of the cross over them. If the legend has been embellished, it is still in the spirit of St. Francis. Lovingly he called the animals his brothers, which is itself highly indicative. How he loved the lambs, which were for him symbolic of the Lamb of God, who takes away the sins of the world! How closely he was drawn to the larks who joyously soar up into the sky! With wonderful tenderness he lifted the little worms off the path and carried them to safety, so that no traveller should tread on them. There were of course exceptions. St. Francis had no love for ants — they worked too hard! Their endless activity — a symbol of the present day mad rush — seemed to him like greed. Basically the animals were for St. Francis part of the holy mystery, because all living things had been purchased by the sacrifice on Golgotha. He wanted a special decree to be issued by the Emperor that at Christmas people should scatter corn and other food for birds in front of their houses, so that the birds should also have some sense of the festive season.

People have always noticed St. Francis' relationship to nature, but they have seldom understood it properly. It has nothing to do with going into raptures over nature, because this is blind to the difficult problems with which nature's contradictions confront us. Much more it was because the heart of the saint was moved with compassion for all creatures. He guessed the secrets of the created world, and he thought of the salvation of the whole of nature. "In some marvellous way which was barred to other men, he found the entry into the secret of things," wrote an eyewitness. St. Francis saw the true reality of the created world, which the rest of us are capable of grasping only in parables. The reflection of the image of God in everything could be detected in all that he said. A repetition of Paradise, when all the animals came to Adam and he gave each of them a name, lies in St. Francis' attitude to dumb creatures. He was not concerned with making them subject to him and lording it over them, an attitude which mankind has wantonly abused and which has brought untold suffering upon the animal kingdom. He thought of animals as his brothers in a unique way, which can only be understood with New Testament simplicity and even then this brotherhood can be grasped at best with the heart. Alas, Christians have not followed this approach. Perhaps they have been unable to do so, for this is a matter of grace and not of the will. This affection for all forms of life is like the dawning of a new day in human history.

St. Francis' "Canticle of the Sun" probably reflects most suggestively the picture of his relationship to all living things:

> All creatures of our God and King,
> Lift up your voice and with us sing
> Alleluia, Alleluia!
> Thou burning sun with golden beam,
> Thou silver moon with softer gleam,
>   O praise Him, O praise Him,
>   Alleluia, Alleluia, Alleluia!
>
> Thou rushing wind that art so strong,
> Ye clouds that sail in heaven along,
> O praise Him, Alleluia!
> Thou rising morn, in praise rejoice,
> Ye lights of evening, find a voice.
>
> Thou flowing water, pure and clear,
> Make music for thy Lord to hear,
> Alleluia, Alleluia!

Thou fire so masterful and bright,
That givest man both warmth and light.

Dear mother earth, who day by day
Unfoldest blessings on our way,
O praise Him, Alleluia!
The flowers and fruits that in thee grow,
Let them His glory also show.

And all ye men of tender heart,
Forgiving others, take your part,
O sing ye, Alleluia!
Ye who long pain and sorrow bear,
Praise God and on Him cast your care.
And thou, most kind and gentle death,
Waiting to hush our latest breath,
O praise Him, Alleluia!
Thou leadest home the child of God,
And Christ our Lord the way hath trod.

Let all things their Creator bless,
And worship Him in humbleness,
O praise Him, Alleluia!
Praise, praise the Father, praise the Son,
And praise the Spirit, Three in One.

Translation by William Henry Draper, 1855-1933.

The saint himself often sang this hymn. It is a splendid song of praise, yet it is but a miserable stammer compared with what lived in him. If we read the "Canticle of the Sun" aloud several times, we can sense how poetically St. Francis has steeped himself in heavenly goodwill. Form and content have become one. His inspired nature had to express itself in verse and song. Poetry was for him a heavenly message which he welcomed in song. He called himself one of God's minstrels; his gaiety was part of that. Francis was by no means the only songster in the Franciscan brotherhood. He had imitators in this too; one has only to think of the splendid hymns of Jacopone da Todi, in which one cannot become engrossed without experiencing an inward joy.

The "Canticle of the Sun" is the greatest and purest song of praise that teaches us, as we sing it, how to glorify God. It is a unique hymn to his glory and must never be understood in any kind of pantheistic way, since Francis always reckoned Nature to be God's creation. The Poverello accepted the invitation of the psalmist to "praise the Lord" and did indeed praise him with his whole heart. In his hymn he proclaims that praise, glory, and honor belong to God alone, whose name no man is worthy to pronounce. St. Francis saw God's created world, felt its creatureliness and celebrated the sun above all. He himself radiated light and warmth, spoke of Brother Sun, and recognized it as a symbol of the Almighty. Then he thought of all creatures whom he always addressed as brothers, was sensitive to wind, weather and air, water and fire, the whole earth as mother of all, with its fruits, flowers, and herbs, and he did not forget the men who out of sheer love practice forgiveness and abide in peace. Lastly death, the dreaded skeleton, received the title of brother, and the last word was once more praise, glory, and thanksgiving "in great humility." The Hymn to the Sun is inexhaustible: it cannot be expressed in words, least of all should it be interpreted in terms of theology. It is more than all theology put together, it is faith, it is mysticism, it is an association with God.

St. Francis and St. Clare

Over and above the unique sweetness of St. Francis, which is to be savored in his joyfulness, his love of peace, and his relationship to nature, we must not forget the fearful strictness of the unconditional imitation of Christ, from which it springs. Different contrasts were united in St. Francis. It would give a distorted picture if we were to stress one side at the expense of the other. The wholly sweet harmony of his spirit, of which Brother Leo has written, was able to resolve contradictions and to endow his nature with vast and not easily soluble tensions.

With regard to St. Francis' relationship with women — as Celano emphasizes in his second biography — he warned against any familiarity with women, he, who himself was able to recall the features of only two women. Probably Francis occasionally expressed himself in this way and in so doing paid his tribute to the mediaeval monkish attitude. Anyone who presses St. Francis' words in this connection too far, gets a picture of an unnatural personality which is far from accurate. In his heart the little brother from Assisi had a much more intuitive, happier attitude to women: one has only to think of his tender understanding with St. Clare. The young noblewoman had decided to follow St. Francis, but it was impossible for her to take to the road with him and his brothers. After St. Clare's secret flight from the home of her parents she met Francis, who cut off her hair as the sign of her induction. He then took her to a Benedictine convent and finally found her a suitable place in San Damiano, where she could live the penniless life of Christ. St. Clare was a quite extraordinary woman. With feminine intuition she understood perfectly and to the uttermost the idea of poverty and remained true to it without wavering. Even when the brothers withdrew from it, she remained steadfast and allowed nothing to deflect her from it. "Holy Father, I wish in no way, now or ever, to have a dispensation from the imitation of Christ." This was her splendid reply to the pope, which all the members of the Order had to repeat after her.

Between Francis and Clare there was an unusually tender relationship. On the rare occasions of his visits she entertained him with feminine attentiveness: flowers on the table during their scanty meals were but a small indication of this. The "radiant one" — which is the meaning of the name Clare — outlived Francis by many years, yet she had only one ambition — to live as St. Francis had lived. There are many beautiful legends about the mystical relationship between St. Francis and St. Clare which illuminate the essence of this association.

It was only to be expected that people began to whisper about the relationship between Francis and Clare, at all events Francis heard of more than one improper insinuation. St. Francis then said to St. Clare: "Sister, do you know what people are saying about us?"

St. Clare did not reply. Her heart failed her, and she felt that if she were to speak she would burst into tears.

At length St. Francis said: "It is time for us to part. You must be in the convent by nightfall. I shall go alone and follow at a distance as God guides me." St. Clare fell on her knees in the middle of the road, pulled herself together after a while, stood up and went on with bowed head without a backward look. The road led through a wood. But she did not have the strength to go on, without comfort and hope, without a word of farewell from him. She waited. "Father," she said, "when shall we see each other again?"

"When summer returns, when the roses are in bloom," he replied. Then something wonderful happened. Suddenly it seemed to him as if a mass of roses sprang into bloom on the juniper bushes and thickly covered hedges. After her initial astonishment St. Clare hurried forward, plucked a bunch of roses and put it in St. Francis' hands. From that day onward St. Francis and St. Clare were never separated.

This is the language of legend, which holds a beauty which the language of history never captures. This is why we cannot disregard the language of legend, however many objections may be raised against it. "Never again were Francis and Clare separated," says the legend, and what else does that mean than that they were so closely united through the life of Christ that neither time nor space came between them.

A second legendary tale concerns the inward relationship between these two and clothes it in words which sparkle like precious stones.

St. Francis was once deeply concerned about how St. Clare was faring since she had such a heavy burden to bear through her love of poverty. Worried and tired he stumbled on until his feet almost sank into the ground. He dragged himself to a fountain which bubbled with fresh water and formed a clear surface in the trough into which the jet from the fountain outlet fell. For a long time the man of God stood bowed over the fountain. Then he raised his head and said happily to Brother Leo: "Brother Leo, little lamb of God, what do you think I have seen in the water of the fountain?" "The moon, Father, which is reflected in it," replied the brother.

"No, Brother Leo, it is not our brother Moon that I have seen in the water of the fountain, but by the merciful grace of God I have seen the very face of our Sister Clare, and it was so pure and radiant with holy joy, that all my misgivings were suddenly banished, and I received an assurance that our sister at this very moment is enjoying that deep joy which God keeps for his favorites, in that he heaps upon them the treasures of poverty." The spiritual bond of prayer between Francis and Clare overcame all spatial remoteness, since it depended on the inward state of mind of each other.

People have spoken of the sublime love between Francis and Clare, "that was free from all animal urges, but not free from a genuine man-woman relationship." This definition. hardly meets the case. St. Francis loved St. Clare not as a woman, but as the being who most completely incarnated the poor life of Christ. The love which bound these two together was of a purity, a spirituality, and a Christ-likeness which went beyond any definition.

The "Little Flowers" describe this shared experience. "While they sat there enraptured with hands and eyes lifted towards heaven, it seemed to the citizens of Assisi and Bettona and along the whole route, as if the church of St. Mary of the Angels together with the huts of the brothers and the forest which at that time encircled the settlement, were standing in the midst of bright flames — everything appeared to be enveloped in a huge fire. People hastened from Assisi to bring help; for they really believed that everything was going up in flames. When they reached the spot, however, they found everything intact and unharmed. And as they went in they found the blessed Francis with St. Clare and all the brothers in a state of God-given rapture, sitting humbly at table and seized by a power from on high." Only when one has seen these flames, does one begin to understand the relationship between St. Francis and St. Clare. Until then everything remains on the level of unseemly popular gossip, referred to in the legend, and only afterwards does one begin to sense something of the totally different spiritual posibilities of the saints.

The Battle for the Order

Although Francis produced an indefinable aura, he was not spared from life's tragic side, which at first seems surprising in this man of sweetness. Elias of Cortona, a highly complex character, succeeded in ingratiating himself with Francis but at the same time gradually but steadfastly wrested the brotherhood out of his hands. This ambitious man seized the leadership of the Order, changed its direction by introducing innovations which gave rise to much confusion within the Order. They rebelled against Francis: "We no longer want you as our leader! You are no orator, your appearance is insignificant, and you have a simple mind." The Poverello did not want to go against the brothers and was anxious to resolve all difficulties with humility and without falling back on ecclesiastical authority.

Francis resigned from the leadership of the Order with a heavy heart. A groan burst from him as he exclaimed sadly: "Woe betide the brothers who are my adversaries. . . . Who are those men who have snatched my Order and my brothers out of my hands?" Francis would have nothing to do with open resistance. He would not allow things to develop into a bitter quarrel with Elias but submitted humbly, and with the deepest sorrow gave up his dearest task. Elias seized the reins, made the humble brotherhood into an Order capable of coping with the outside world and one which was later to supply university professors, but who became so involved in things and so arrogant, that finally when he died it was as an excommunicated Christian outside the Church. Meanwhile Francis retired from the scene, remembered his beginnings, quietly and diffidently cared for the lepers, and received heaven's richest reward.

We must not oversimplify the conflict between Francis and Elias. It was not merely a question of rivalry, for there were many brothers on the side of Elias who were pressing for a more academic approach. Francis did not reject scholarly studies out of hand. He respected scholars and carefully preserved everything in writing. But his little brothers must not become scholars, because according to him knowledge inflates the ego. We must therefore put a question mark against a Franciscan theology. Francis' anathema against the provincial minister in Bologna may not be ignored. The saint feared the ambition of the scholars and believed that in times of affliction learned brothers would hardly stand the test. "Many are inclined, supposedly on account of being of more use to society, to abandon their true vocation, namely a purely religious simplicity, prayer, and inwardness, together with our Lady Poverty. In so doing they believe that through deeper understanding of the Scriptures they will come to a more intense piety and love of God; in reality they will in this way only become inwardly cold and empty." Francis' simplicity is not to be equated with primitiveness; much more it possesses the profundity of the gospel, which cannot be arrived at through scholarship.

The problem was made more acute by the Curia, because it supported the efforts of Elias of Cortona. The spirit did not keep pace with the rapid growth of the Order, or in modern terms, numbers create new problems, which the Curia perhaps saw more clearly than St. Francis. "We must also think of those who will come after you," said the pope, a realistic approach which, it must be allowed, has a certain justification. The charismatic Poverello on the contrary relied wholly on the guidance of the Spirit, and knew exactly how much a man can endure. Nevertheless he cried out at one time in anguish: "My God, what will happen after my death to the poor family which of your goodness you have entrusted to me, sinner that I am?" Full of dark forebodings he wandered around until an angel gave him the assurance: "I tell you in the name of God, your Order will never end until the Day of Judgment." The anxiety and the angelic message have been proved true until the present day and are a comfort to many of the Little Brothers in the present time.

Looking at this conflict one cannot say that Francis was on the side of light and that Elias was on the side of darkness. Rather both sides were right, Francis with his faith that could move mountains, and the Curia together with Elias, which recognized human weakness. We may ask which of the two parties was more in the right. The tragic side of the argument lies in the fact that Francis and Elias had both seen different aspects of the truth. But this was a Christian drama, which was different from a Greek tragedy, in which at the end man is silent in his agony, whereas despite all his difficulties the vault of heaven soared above St. Francis.

Likeness to Christ

After Francis had withdrawn from the leadership of the Order, more and more he sought solitude. He loved the jagged rocks of Mt. La Verna where he was granted a vision about which one hardly dares to speak. St. Francis saw a seraph with six wings hovering above him, who with outstretched hands and closed feet was fixed to the Cross. The saint was seized with deep amazement at this vision but was unable to interpret it. "Suddenly traces of woundprints began to be visible on his hands and feet as he had seen them shortly before on the crucified man above him." The Poverello had, like no Christian before him, received the woundprints of the Lord, a gift of grace which is beyond discussion.

St. Francis spoke little and only "cautiously as in riddles" about the mysterious stigmata and said: "Blessed is the man who can keep the secrets of the Lord his God within him." There is really no doubt about the stigmata: they are well attested. In the "Little Flowers" it says: "Why the woundprints appeared on St. Francis is not wholly clear." If the authors of the "Little Flowers" were puzzled, how much more must the man of today confess his incompetence in this matter. One can only guess cautiously that it was an acknowledgement of the saint by Christ. St. Francis' likeness to Christ had also its outward expression: his mystical union with Christ reached such a pitch that it became also physical. The stigmata are a sign, like the "sign of Jonah" of which Christ spoke, that we ought to leave unexplained.

After this mystical experience Francis commended the holy mountain to the special protection of the brothers, and bade them see to it that this place should never be allowed to be used for profane purposes. Then the Poverello spoke the words of farewell full of saintly sadness, words that once more are only recorded in the "Little Flowers": "Farewell, Brother Masseo, farewell! Go in peace, dear sons! Farewell! I leave you in my body, but my heart remains here." These words of St. Francis are certainly true. Something of his soul has remained behind, something inexpressible, which will be felt for all time. It is also still invisibly present, though we can sense its gentle presence.

Brother Death

After this climax it was only a case of waiting for the end. St. Francis in his last years was a sick man. Weakened by his strict asceticism and by the stigmata, he was hardly able to walk. A donkey bore him from place to place. His eyes began to give him trouble so that he could not face the light of day for several weeks. The doctor thought an operation was necessary and seared him from the temples to the eyebrows with a red hot iron. Francis maintained that he felt no heat. This barbaric torture did him no good. For the saint there was no frontier between pleasure and pain; they both melted into one another, and both stimulated him to sing the praises of the Almighty. Francis knew that "the illness of the body benefits the soul if one accepts it with resignation."

At the early age of forty-two he felt the approach of death. There was no trace of fear and horror as death drew near. He blessed once more his beloved town of Assisi and in his last hour had himself laid naked on the bare ground, for "he wanted to fight naked with the naked." Then he said: "Welcome, Brother Death" and commanded Brother Angelo and Brother Leo to sing to him of Brother Death. He himself added these lines to the "Canticle of the Sun":

> "Praised be thou, Lord,
> Through our beloved brother, Death;
> No living creature can escape him.

Woe to those who die in their grievous sins!
Blessed are those whom he finds doing thy most holy will!
For the second death will not harm them."

St. Francis welcomed Brother Death with a hymn on his lips. A more Christian death is not possible. His ardent desire: "Strike then, O longed for hour" was granted when he embraced sweet death on October 3, 1226.

Soon after his death solemn consultations took place about his canonization. No doubts were expressed. The unanimous verdict was: "The utterly holy life of this totally saintly man needs no confirmation by miracles. We have seen it with our own eyes, handled it, as it were, with our own hands, and verified it in the light of truth." Of this the whole of Christendom was convinced, both then and still today.

Mission and Influence

St. Francis' outward appearance was not particularly impressive. Celano described him as a man with a happy face and a good expression. "Not very tall, rather on the small side, he had a medium sized round head, a rather long and mobile face, a flat low brow; not particularly large, black, clear eyes, dark hair, straight eyebrows, a regular, fine straight nose tilting upwards, small ears, flat temples, an attractive, passionate and pungent mode of speech, a strong, pleasing, clear and resonant voice, close, even, white teeth, thin soft lips, a black cropped beard, a slender neck, straight shoulders, short arms, soft hands, long fingers, rather protruding nails, thin legs, very small feet, a soft skin; he was very thin, wore a rough habit, needed very little sleep, had a very generous hand." Brother Masseo said to Francis outright: "You are no beauty." That was a fair verdict. Francis was full of a different inward beauty, and this is what made him so lovable.

Intrinsically Francis was "no scholar, but he was instructed by God in that wisdom which comes from above. . . . His pure spirit pierced into the heart of things whereas learned scholarship remains on the surface. . . . But not every kind of simplicity found approval from him, only that for which God alone is sufficient." As has been previously noted, no one can pretend to have uncovered the "true motives and intentions of St. Francis." We are all faced with a riddle and should be on our guard against attributing to him our own views. Francis never allows himself to be comprehended, but one can come close to him, yet never close enough.

His mission flowed from his inmost being. Francis' message consisted in his likeness to Christ, which appears once more in his will, although Bonaventure in his biography which was approved by the Order makes no further mention of it. Francis was not merely the Christ-symbol of the Middle Ages, but has reminded every generation of the Lord with unparalleled forcefulness, a passionate incarnation of him which is far greater than any development of a program today. One cannot seriously become involved with the Poverello without getting Christ constantly brought before one's eyes. According to Brother Leo, Francis "has been transformed into Christ, thanks to his perfect imitation of Christ through holy humility." This statement is no exaggeration, for this is the goal of every Christian who would say with St. Paul: "Not I but Christ who lives in me." Francis came close to the Lord as no one else has done since the time of the apostles. He brought Christ once more into the world and achieved a renewal of the presence of Christ.

Corresponding to his mission was his enormous influence. According to contemporary reports Christians before Francis had become indifferent, their love to God had become a dead thing, and awe in fact of his majestic presence had disappeared. A frightful godlessness had taken control of mankind, with thoughts only of money, pleasure, and sin.

Then Francis appeared and everything was changed from the foundations. The preface to the "Legend of the Three Companions" gives this change eloquent expression: "Shining like the early dawn and like the morning star, as the rising sun floods the world with glowing streams of light and makes it fruitful, so Francis burst upon the world like a new kind of light. When this sun rose the world lay to some extent frozen in winter's frost, in darkness and barren of life. His words and his deeds were like a beautiful radiance; truth shines forth, love is kindled, virtue, mother of many achievements, has the power to awaken a new and more beautiful kind of life. The three societies which he founded blossom like a garden full of all sorts of trees laden with fruit. What amazing fruitfulness! It was the entry of spring into the world." This splendid description sums up St. Francis: he can only be compared with the rising sun and the onset of spring!

After his death a sadness descended on the world, which resulted in new wars and famines. Great misery came over the earth which St. Francis in his day had been able to check.

Is this a contemporary exaggeration, originating from his enthusiastic followers? They have never allowed themselves to be carried away by their own words. Even in our own day St. Francis has been regarded in the same way; out of the many tributes we may select three wholly independent testimonies.

Nicholas Berdyaev, the religious philosopher, in his autobiography, called St. Francis "the most important man to appear in the history of Christianity." This judgement is all the more significant inasmuch as it comes from a Russian thinker who did not belong to the Catholic Church. In fact, one can hardly be sufficiently concerned with "the most important man to appear in the history of Christianity," for Christendom has never worked this out in all its fullness.

Reinhold Schneider had similar thoughts about St. Francis. According to him the Poverello was destined to begin the realization of the Word and his deepest originality was to obey the Lord's words: "The unique and truly Franciscan essence lies in the courage to embrace the absolute with all its logical consequences. It does not lie in a new idea or a new feeling, but in the fact that a life was lived in obedience to Christ with the utmost seriousness; in the incredible boldness of the demand to be transformed into Christ by the way of humble imitation." So St. Francis is for the poet the living embodiment of the answer to the question as to the meaning of western Christianity. Reinhold Schneider has repeatedly dealt with the Poverello: like few people the poet was aware of the "hour of St. Francis."

Julien Green too, whose profound novels describe the remoteness from God of modern man, expressed in his perceptive diaries the visionary insight: "Over the last few days I have been asking myself whether Christ has not given us a second gospel in the life of St. Francis." It is quite evident that in all these tributes some ideas of the saintliness of Francis is given which will attract present day people into its orbit.

What the philosophers and poets have thought about St. Francis is at the same time beautiful and profound. He himself expressed his joy in many ways: "He often used to pick a block of wood off the ground, laid it on his left arm, took a stick in his right hand to serve as a bow and drew is across the log as if he were playing a fiddle or some other instrument. Then he moved about in the appropriate rhythm and sang a French song about the Lord Jesus Christ. In the end all these songs and dances used to finish up in tears of emotion as he thought of Christ, and he was filled with sheer happiness. He forgot what he had in his hands and was carried into heaven." A wonderful picture of a unique beauty! In such a scene one seems to feel the sharp sweetness as something tangible, and to hear the plea to take the Franciscan fiddle into one's hands and play to a bewildered world that ancient and yet ever new melody which the human heart cannot resist.

His Will

1. The Lord has granted it to me, Brother Francis, to begin my life in penitence: for as I was still in my sins it seemed to me intolerably bitter to look upon lepers. And the Lord himself led me in among them, and I had compassion on them. And when I left them, what had seemed to me bitter was changed into sweetness of soul and body. Thereafter it was but a short time before I left the world.

2. And the Lord granted me in the churches such a faith that I prayed in all simplicity, saying: "We adore you, Lord Jesus Christ — and in all your churches throughout the world, and we thank you that you have redeemed the world by your sacred Cross."

3. Further, the Lord gave and still gives me such great trust by virtue of their ordination in the priests who live in accordance with the rules of the holy Roman Church, that even if they were to persecute me I should still turn to them for refuge. And if I possessed the wisdom of Solomon, and found poor priests of this world, in the parishes in which they live, I will not preach without their permission. And to them and to all others will I show reverence, will love them and honor them as my masters. And I will disregard their sins, because I see the Son of God in them and they are my masters. And I do this because in this world I see nothing of him, the highest Son of God in physical form apart from his most holy body and his most holy blood, which these men receive and which they alone pass on to others. And I wish that these holy mysteries should be honored above all, worshipped, and preserved in costly places. I will collect inscriptions of his most holy name and of his words whenever I find them in unseemly places, and I beg that they be collected and deposited in honored places. And we must respect all theologians and those who instruct us in the most holy words of God, and we must show them reverence as men who bestow on us spirit and life.

4. And after the Lord had given me brothers, no one showed me what I had to do, but the Almighty himself revealed to me that I must live in accordance with the holy gospel. And I caused it to be written down in few and simple words and the pope himself confirmed it. And those who came to share this life gave all that they had to the poor. And they were content with a habit, a cord, and breeches. And we wished for no more. Those of us who were clergy said the daily offices like other clergy, the laymen said the Lord's prayer. We gladly frequented the churches. And we were uneducated and subject to everyone.

5. And I work with my hands, and want to work. And I want to emphasize that all

the other brothers should undertake some honorable work. Those who cannot do that should learn, not from a desire to earn money, but to set an example and to banish idleness. And if on occasion we get no pay for our work, then we take refuge at the Lord's table and beg for alms from door to door.

6. As a greeting, the Lord has revealed to me that we should say: "The Lord give you peace."

7. The brothers must take care not to accept under any circumstances churches, modest dwellings, and anything that is built for them, if they do not fit in with the holy poverty which we have promised in the Rule: we are there always only for a short while as strangers and pilgrims.

8. I strictly enjoin all brothers in obedience, wherever they may be, that they should not dare to ask the Roman Curia for any kind of letter of safe conduct, neither themselves or through an intermediary, nor for a church, nor for any other place, nor on the pretext of preaching, nor on account of bodily persecution. Rather they must in cases where they are not well received, flee to another region, and do penance there with God's blessing.

9. And it is my firm purpose to obey the minister general of this brotherhood, and that guardian whom he chooses to give me according to his judgment. And I shall be in this sense a prisoner in his hands, that I can do nothing and go nowhere without obedience towards him and without his approval, because he is my master. And although I am foolish and sick, I will always have a priest to say the office for me, as it says in the Rule.

10. And all the other brothers shall be bound likewise to obey their guardians and to say the daily offices as the Rule prescribes. And if any be found who have not been saying their prayers at the daily offices in accordance with the Rule and wanted to introduce a different system or were not good Catholics — all brothers, whoever they may be, shall in obedience be bound to take such a man wherever they find him to the nearest custodian of the place where they have found him. And the custodian shall be under strictest obedience to guard him closely like a prisoner day and night, so that he cannot be snatched out of his hands until he has personally handed him over to the custody of his minister. And the minister shall be bound in strictest obedience to despatch him in the charge of such brothers as will guard him day and night like a prisoner, until they have delivered him to the Bishop of Ostia, who is the head of the whole brotherhood and keeps it under his protection and discipline.

11.   And the brothers must not say: "This is a different Rule," for this is a reminder, an admonition, and an encouragement and my will and testament, that I, the quite unimportant Brother Francis make for you, my blessed brothers, in order that we may as better Catholics observe the Rule that we have promised the Lord to keep.

12.   And the minister general and all other ministers and guardians shall be bound in obedience not to add or subtract anything to or from these words. And at all times they shall keep this document together with the Rule in their possession. And at all chapters which they hold they shall read these words as well when they read the Rule. And I strictly enjoin my brothers, both clerical and lay, to be obedient in adding no explanations to the Rule or to this document, saying: "This is what it means." But as the Lord has charged me to say and to write the Rule and these words plainly and clearly, so must you understand them plainly and without explanation and observe them with holy effectiveness right to the end.

13.   And each and every one who observes this, will in heaven be filled with the blessing of the all-highest Father, and on earth will be filled with the blessing of his beloved Son, in communion with the Holy Spirit, the Comforter, and with all the powers of Heaven and of all the saints. And I, Brother Francis, your totally unimportant servant, confirm to you as much as I can both inwardly and outwardly this most holy blessing.

THE WORLD OF ST. FRANCIS

Excerpts from the Lives of St. Francis
by Thomas of Celano, Bonaventure, and the
Three Companions (English Translation
from *St. Francis of Assisi, Writings and
Early Biographies, English Omnibus of the
Sources for the Life of St. Francis*) with
71 color photographs by Toni Schneiders.

The Young Francis

1   View of Assisi

Assisi, a town in the valley of Spoleto, was the home of Francis, the son of Pietro Bernadone, a cloth-merchant, who was wholly intent on making money.

2   Lane in Assisi with the "Stalleta," in which Francis is said to have been born

Francis' mother Pica was an excellent woman; and like another Elizabeth, she gave birth to her blessed son in the absence of his father who had gone to France on business. She wished the child to be called John. When Peter returned from France, he insisted that his son should be called Francis after the country he had recently left.

(Legend of the Three Companions, 1)

3   Troubadours

He was the admiration of all and strove to outdo the rest in the pomp of vainglory, in jokes, in strange doings, in idle and useless talk, in songs, in soft and flowing garments, for he was very rich.

(Thomas of Celano, First Life, 2)

4   "Rocca Maggiore," the Fortress above Assisi

5   The Town Hall of Perugia, the nearby town hostile to Assisi

6   A man pays homage to the young Francis on the marketplace of Assisi

His good life, his gentleness and patience, his almost superhuman readiness to oblige, together with his generosity which exceeded his means, and his pleasant manner were distinguishing features which marked him out as a young man. They seemed to be almost a foretaste of things to come, indicating that the abundance of God's blessings would be heaped upon him more plentifully than ever in the future. Indeed, one citizen of the town, a very simple man who appears to have been inspired by God, took off his cloak when he met Francis in Assisi one day and spread it under his feet, saying that he deserved the respect of everybody because he would do great things and be honored by the whole Church.

(Bonaventure, Major Life of St. Francis, I, 1)

7   Façade of the Roman Temple of Minerva on the marketplace of Assisi

Indeed, once when there was a bloody battle between the citizens of Perugia and those of Assisi, Francis was made captive with several others and endured the squalor of a prison. His fellow captives were plunged in sorrow, bemoaning miserably their imprisonment; but Francis rejoiced in the Lord, laughed at his chains and despised them. His grieving companions resented his happiness and considered him mad. Francis replied prophetically: "Why do you think I rejoice? I will yet be venerated as a saint throughout the whole world." And so it has truly come about; everything he said has been fulfilled.

(Thomas of Celano, *Second Life,* 4)

The Call of St. Francis —
Founding of the First Order

9   View of Spoleto

Francis was still ignorant of God's plan for him and he prepared to enlist with a high-ranking knight in Apulia, in the hope of acquiring distinction as a soldier in his service, as his vision seemed to indicate. He set out shortly afterwards but when he reached the next town (Spoleto), he heard God calling him by his first name as he lay asleep, and saying, "Francis, who can do more for you, a lord or his servant, a rich man or a beggar?" When he replied that a lord or a rich man could do more, he was asked, "Then why are you abandoning the Lord to devote yourself to a servant? Why are you choosing a beggar instead of God who is infinitely rich?" "Lord," replied Francis, "what will you have me do?" And God told him, "Go back to your own town."

(Bonaventure, *Major Life,* I, 2)

10   Francis gives his cloak to a poor knight

Once he met a knight who was of noble birth but very poor, so that he was not properly clad. Francis felt sorry for him and immediately took off his own cloak and gave it to him.

(Bonaventure, *Major Life,* I, 2)

11   View of San Damiano

When Francis returned to Assisi, he discovered a certain church along the road that had been built in honor of St. Damian but which was now threatening to collapse because it was so old. When this new soldier of Christ came up to this church, moved with pity over such great need, he entered it with fear and reverence. And when he found there a certain poor priest, he kissed his sacred hands with great faith, and offered him the money he had with him, asking his permission to live there.

(Thomas of Celano, *First Life,* 8-9)

12   Francis prays before the cross in San Damiano

There, as he knelt in prayer before a painted image of the Crucified, he felt greatly comforted in spirit and his eyes were full of tears as he gazed at the cross. Then, all of a sudden, he heard a voice coming from the cross and telling him three times, "Francis, go and repair my house. You see it is falling down." Francis was alone in the church and he was terrified at the sound of the voice, but the power of its message penetrated his heart and he went into an ecstasy. Eventually, he came back to himself and prepared to obey the command he had received. He was quite willing to devote himself entirely to repairing the ruined church of San Damiano, although the message really referred to the universal Church which Christ won for himself at the price of his own blood.

(Bonaventure, *Major Life,* II, 1)

13   The cross of San Damiano

14   View of the cathedral of San Rufino in Assisi

15   Francis cuts himself off from his father

But when his father saw that he could not dissuade him from the way he had chosen, he was determined by all means to get his money back. He brought his son before the bishop of the city, so that, he might renounce all his possessions into his hands, and give back everything he had. In his genuine love for poverty, Francis was more than ready to comply and he willingly appeared before the bishop. There, without hesitation, he immediately took off his clothes and gave them back to his father. He even took off his trousers in his fervor and enthusiasm and stood there naked before them all. Then he said to his father, "Until now I called you my father, but from now on I can say without reserve, 'Our Father who are in heaven.' He is all my wealth and I place all my confidence in him." When the bishop heard this, he was amazed at his passionate fervor. He jumped to his feet and took Francis into his embrace, covering him with the cloak he was wearing, like the good man that he was. Then he told his servants to bring some clothes for him and they gave him an old tunic which belonged to one of the bishop's farmhands. Francis took it gratefully and drew a cross on it with his own hand with a piece of chalk, making it a worthy garment for a man who was crucified and a beggar. And so the servant of the most high King was left stripped of all that belonged to him, that he might follow the Lord whom he loved, who hung naked on the cross.

(Thomas of Celano, *First Life,* 14; and Bonaventure, *Major Life,* II, 4 (abridged))

16   Ruins of a Romanesque chapel

Francis remembered again the command he had received from the cross to repair the church of San Damiano. For love of Christ, poor and crucified, he overcame his embarrassment and begged from those who had known him as a wealthy young man, and he loaded himself with stones, although he was weak and worn out with fasting. With God's help and the cooperation of the townspeople he eventually finished the work at San Damiano. Then, in order to avoid becoming lazy, he set about repairing another church dedicated to St. Peter, which was situated farther away from the town.

17   The Chapel of the Porziuncola

When he had finished there, he went to a place called the Porziuncola where there was an old church dedicated to the Virgin Mother of God which was now abandoned with no one to look after it. He loved this spot more than any other in the world. This was the place where St. Francis founded the Order of Friars Minor by divine inspiration. Francis was at Mass one day on the feast of one of the apostles and the passage of the Gospel where our Lord sends out his disciples to preach and tells them how they are to live according to the gospel was read. When Francis heard that they were not to provide gold or silver or copper to fill their purses, that they were not to have a wallet for the journey or a second coat, no shoes or staff, he was overjoyed. He grasped the meaning of the passage immediately in his love for apostolic poverty and committed it to memory. "This is what I want," he exclaimed. "This is what I long for with all my heart." There and then he took off his shoes and laid aside his staff. He conceived a horror of money or wealth of any kind and he wore only one tunic, changing his leather belt for a rope.

(Bonaventure, *Major Life,* II, 8 and III, 1 (abridged))

18 Francis cares for a cripple

All who were afflicted by any bodily suffering received Francis' compassionate love.

19 Franciscans preaching

From then on Francis began to preach penance to all with great fervor of spirit and joy of mind, edifying his hearers with his simple words and his greatness of heart. His words were like a burning fire, penetrating the inmost reaches of the heart, and it filled the minds of all the hearers with admiration. In all his preaching, before he expounded the word of God to those gathered about, he first prayed for peace for them, saying: "The Lord give you peace."

(Thomas of Celano, *First Life,* 23 (abridged))

20 Belfry of San Stefano in Assisi

Expansion of the Order — the Second Order

21 View of the town of Trevi

When he saw that the number of friars was slowly increasing, Francis wrote a short, simple, rule of life for himself and his companions. This was based on an unshakable foundation, the following of the gospel, and to this he added a limited number of other directions such as seemed necessary for their life in common. He was anxious to have what he had written approved by the pope, and so, placing all his trust in God's guidance, he decided to present himself with his companions before the Apostolic See.

(Bonaventure, *Major Life,* III, 8)

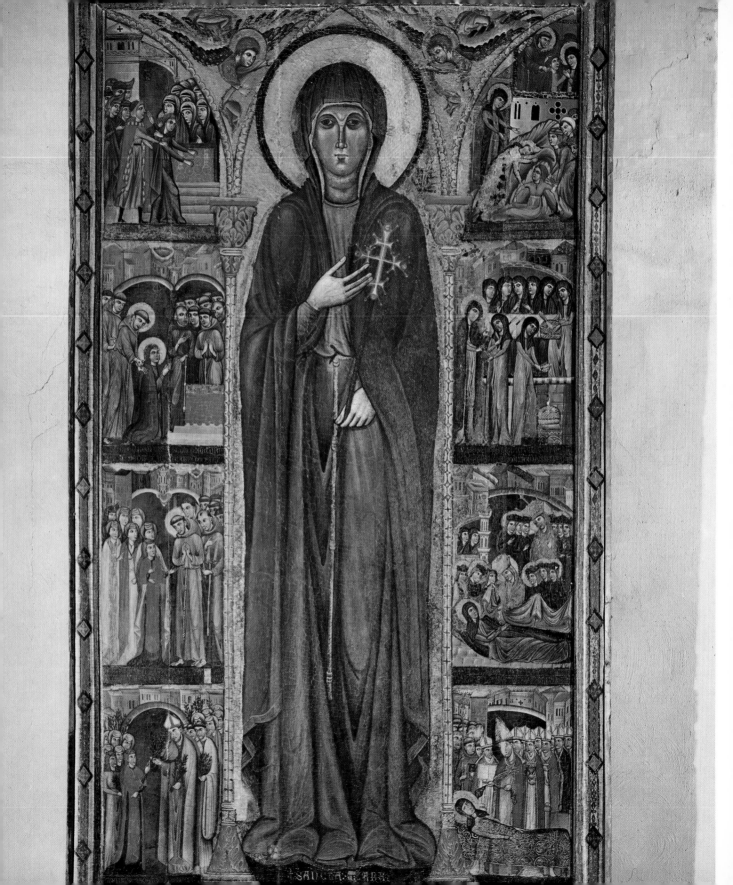

SANCTA CLARA

...ua si mat̃ nutrit et diligit filium suũ carnalem, quanto diligentius debet qui diligere et nutrire fr̃em suum spirituale.

Si qui fr̃um instigante inimico mortalit̃ peccauerint, pro illis peccatis de quib; ordinatũ fuerit int̃ fr̃es ut ñ...
 si pb̃ri sunt cum misericordia iniungant illis penitentiam. Si uero pb̃ri non sunt iniung̃ faciant p alios sacerdotes...
...nicũ. quia ira ⁊ conturbatio in se et in aliis impediunt caritatem. De electione generalis minist̃ri huius...
...dem minist̃rum et seruum totius frat̃nitatis et ei teneantur firmit̃ obedire. Quo decedente electio successo...
...per insimul conuenire ubicumq; a generali minist̃ro fuit constitutum. et hoc semel in tribus annis...
...uniuersitate minist̃rorum prouincialium et custodum predictum minist̃rum non ee sufficientem ad seruitium et...
Capitulm uero pentecostes minist̃ri et custodes possint singuli si uoluerint et eis expedire uidebitur eosdem...
...us epi cum abeo illis fuerit contradictum. et nullus fr̃um populo penitus audeat predicare nisi a minist̃...
...hortor eosdem fr̃es ut in predicatione quam faciunt sint examinata et casta eor̃ eloquia. ad utilitatem et...
...am feat d̃ns super terram. De ammonitione et correctione fr̃um. fr̃es qui sunt minist̃ri et serui aliorum fr...
...atum suam et regulam ñram. fr̃es uo qui sunt subditi recordentur q̃ propt̃ deum abnegauerint proprias...
...um contraria anime et Regule ñre. Et ubicumq; sunt fr̃es qui scirent et cognoscerent se non posse R...
...ignue eos recipiant et tantam familiaritatem habeant circa ipos ut dicere possint eis et facere...
...ut caueant fr̃es ab omni superbia. uanagl̃a. inuidia. auaritia. cura. et sollicitudine huius seculi de...
...desiderare debent habere spiritum d̃ni et sc̃am eius operationem. orare semper ad eum puro corde et...
...et arguunt quia dicit d̃ns diligite inimicos ũros et orate pro persequentibus et calumpnian...
...seuerauerit usq; in finem hic saluus erit. Quod fr̃es non ingrediantur monasteria monachar̃. p...
...monachar̃ preter illos quibus a sede ap̃lica concessa est licentia specialis. nec fiant compatres uirar̃ ut...
...infideles. Quicumq; fr̃um diuina inspiratione uoluerint ire inter sarracenos et alios infideles pe...
...uideant ee ydoneos admittendum. Ad hoc per obedientiam iniungo minist̃ris ut petant a d̃no pp̃ u...
...per subditi et subiecti pedibus eiusdem sc̃e ecclie stabiles in fide catholica. paupertatem et humilitat...
...am paginam ñre confirmationis infringere ul' ei ausu temerario contraire. Siquis aut̃ hoc attemp...
...Dat̃ Laterañ ... ij ... kl ... Decembr̃ ... pontificat̃ ... ñri

22 *Pope Innocent III's dream*

23 *Pope Innocent blesses Francis and confirms his Rule*

When they arrived at the papal court, Francis was brought before the pope. The Vicar of Christ was in the Lateran palace at the time; and when Francis was announced, he was walking in a hall known as the Mirror Hall, lost in deep thought. He knew nothing about the saint, and so he sent him away indignantly. Francis took his leave with all humility. Later the pope called Francis again and listened to his plans. Then he told him, "My son, pray to Christ that he may show us his will through you. When we are sure of that, we can grant your request without fear." Only a short time before, he had seen a vision from heaven and by divine inspiration he now testified that it would be fulfilled in Francis. As he himself described it, he had a dream in which he saw the Lateran basilica which was threatening to fall being held up by a poor beggarman who put his back to it. "This is certainly the man," he added. "By his work and teaching, he will uphold Christ's Church." As a result of his vision the pope was filled with reverence for Francis and granted his request unconditionally. He always had a special regard for him and, while granting what he asked, he promised to give the friars greater powers in the future. He approved the rule and gave them a mission to preach repentance, conferring the clerical tonsure on the laymen among Francis' companions, so that they could preach the word of God without interference.

(Bonaventure, *Major Life,* III, 9-10 (abridged))

24 *Lane in Assisi*

25 *St. Clare*

26 *Induction of Clare by Francis in the chapel of the Porziuncola*

27 *Clare's refectory in San Damiano*

28 *St. Clare and her life*

San Damiano is the blessed and holy place, where the glorious fellowship and most excellent order of Poor Ladies and holy virgins had its blessed origin about six years after the conversion of St. Francis and through that same blessed man. Of it, the Lady Clare, a native of the city of Assisi, the most precious and the strongest stone of the whole structure, was the foundation. For when, after the beginning of the Order of Brothers, the said lady was converted to God through the counsel of the holy man, she lived to the advantage of many and as an example to a countless multitude. She was of noble parentage, but she was more noble by grace; she was a virgin in body, most chaste in mind; young in age, but mature in spirit; steadfast in purpose and most ardent in her desire for divine love; endowed with wisdom and excelling in humility; Clare by name, more radiant in life, and most radiant in character.

(Thomas of Celano, *First Life,* 18)

29 *Tower of the church of Santa Chiara in Assisi*

30   Francis estabishes peace in Arezzo

31   View of Arezzo

On another occasion St. Francis arrived at Arezzo when the whole town was torn with factions and threatened with destruction. There he was given hospitality in a village near the town and he could see the devils rejoicing over it and urging the people on to mutual slaughter. He was anxious to put the malicious powers of evil to flight and so he sent Brother Silvester, who was a man of dove-like simplicity, telling him to approach the town like a herald. "Go up to the town gate," he said, "and in the name of almighty God command the devils to depart immediately." Silvester did what he was told. He approached the town gate, singing a hymn of praise to God, and there he cried aloud, "In the name of almighty God and by the command of his servant Francis, away with you, all you devils!" There and then the town was restored to peace.

(Bonaventure, *Major Life,* VI, 9)

32   Francis and Dominic

Once when Francis and Dominic met together in Rome, the blessed Dominic asked Francis if he would give him the cord he wore about his waist. Francis at first refused out of humility, but then gave it to him because of his pressing love. Dominic received from him the cord, and girding himself with it beneath his habit, he wore it with great reverence. Finally they joined hands and Dominic declared to Francis, "Brother, I desire that your Order and mine may be one and that we may pursue our life in the Church under the same rule." And when they had left one another, Dominic said to those who were with him, "It is the truth and my strong conviction, that all friars ought to follow this holy man Francis, for his holiness is perfect."

(*Legend of the Three Companions,* 50)

33   The Isola Maggiore on Lake Trasimene

34   The hermitage at Le Carceri near Assisi

35   Hermit's cave near Le Carceri

Therefore the blessed father Francis was being daily filled with the consolation and the grace of the Holy Spirit; and with all vigilance and solicitude he instructed his sons with his new learning, teaching them to walk with undeviating steps the way of holy poverty and blessed simplicity. One day, when he was wondering over the mercy of the Lord with regard to the gifts bestowed upon him, he wished that the future course of his own life and that of his brothers might be shown him by the Lord; he sought out a place of prayer, as he had done so often, and he persevered there for a long time with fear and trembling standing before the Lord of the whole earth, and he thought in the bitterness of his soul of the years he had spent wretchedly, frequently repeating this word: O God, be merciful to me a sinner. Little by little a certain unspeakable joy and very great sweetness began to flood his innermost heart. He was then caught up above himself and absorbed in a certain light; the capacity of his mind was enlarged and he could see clearly what was to come to pass. When this sweetness finally passed, along with the light, renewed in spirit, he seemed changed into another man.

(Thomas of Celano, *First Life,* 26 (abridged))

36   The Bull of Pope Honorius III, in which the Rule of the Order was confirmed

Herald of Christ —
Foundation of the Third Order

37 Portrait of St. Francis

Francis was a most eloquent man, a man of cheerful countenance, of kindly aspect; he was immune to cowardice, free of insolence. He was of medium height, closer to shortness; his head was moderate in size and round, his face a bit long and prominent, his forehead smooth and low; his eyes were of moderate size, black and clear; his hair was black, his eyebrows straight, his nose symmetrical, thin and straight; his ears were upright but small; his temples smooth. His speech was peaceable, fiery, and sharp; his voice was strong, sweet, clear, and sonorous. His teeth were set close together, even, and white; his lips were small and thin; his beard black, but not bushy. His neck was slender, his shoulders straight, his arms short, his hands slender, his fingers long, his nails extended; his legs were thin, his feet small. His skin was delicate, his flesh very spare. He wore rough garments, he slept but very briefly, he gave most generously.

(Thomas of Celano, *First Life*, 83)

38 Ships in the harbor of Ancona

Francis was troubled by a serious problem; and some time afterwards, when he returned from where he had been praying, he put it before the friars who were closest to him, to have it resolved. "What do you think of this, Brothers?" he said. "Which do you think is better? That I should devote all my time to prayer, or that I should go about preaching?" Francis had learned deep secrets from the Teacher of all, but he was a true Friar Minor and he was not ashamed to ask advice from those who were not as advanced as he. He now chose two of the friars and sent them to Brother Silvester; they were to tell him to ask God to solve his problem and send him the answer in God's name. He sent the same message to St. Clare, telling her to pray with her sisters and find our God's will from the holiest and most simple of the sisters who lived under her. By the inspiration of the Holy Spirit Brother Silvester and St. Clare both came to the same conclusion. It was God's will that Francis should go out to preach as a herald of Christ.

(Bonaventure, *Major Life*, XII, 1-2 (much abridged))

39 Francis before the sultan of Egypt

Still his passionate love urged him on, and a third time he set out to preach faith in the Trinity among the pagans by shedding his blood. In the thirteenth year of his religious life he made his way to Syria where he courageously surmounted all dangers in order to reach the presence of the sultan of Egypt. He took with him as his companion a friar named Illuminatus, and he proclaimed to the sultan the triune God and Jesus Christ, the Savior of all, with such steadfastness, with such courage and spirit, that it was clear the promise of the gospel had been fulfilled in him, "I will give you such eloquence and such wisdom as all your adversaries shall not be able to withstand, or to confute" (Lk. 21, 15). When the sultan saw his enthusiasm and courage, he listened to him willingly and pressed him to stay with him. Francis, however, was inspired by God to reply, "If you are willing to become converts to Christ, you and your people, I shall be only too glad to stay with you for love of him. But if you are afraid to abandon the law of Mahomet for Christ's sake, then light a big fire and I will go into it with your priests. That will show you which faith is more sure and more holy." To that the sultan replied, "I do not think that any of my priests would be willing to expose himself to the flames just to defend his faith, or suffer any kind of torture" (he had just caught a glimpse of one of his priests, an old and highly esteemed man, who slipped away the moment he heard Francis' proposal). Then Francis continued "If you are prepared to promise me that you and your people will embrace the Christian religion, if I come out of the fire unharmed, I will enter it alone." The sultan replied that he would not dare to accept a choice like that, for fear of a revolt among his people.

(Bonaventure, *Major Life,* IX, 7-8 (much abridged))

40 Francis is betrothed to Poverty

While he was in this valley of tears, that blessed father considered the common wealth of the sons of men as trifles, and, ambitious for higher things, he longed for poverty with all his heart. Looking upon poverty as especially dear to the Son of God, though it was spurned throughout the whole world, he sought to espouse it in perpetual charity. Therefore, after he had become a lover of her beauty, he not only left his father and mother, but even put aside all things, that he might cling to her more closely as his spouse and that they might be two in one spirit. Therefore he gathered her to himself with chaste embraces and not even for an hour did he allow himself not to be her husband. This, he would tell his sons, is the way to perfection, this the pledge and earnest of eternal riches.

(Thomas of Celano, *Second Life,* 55)

41 Landscape near Poggio Bustone in the valley of Rieti

42 Francis' cave beside the friary of Fonte Colombo, near Rieti

When the Order was already well established and Francis was thinking of having the rule which had been approved by Pope Innocent confirmed for all time by his successor Pope Honorius, God granted him a vision. As a result of this vision Francis decided to shorten the rule which he wanted to have confirmed, because it had become too long by the addition of numerous texts from the gospel. Then he was led by the Holy Spirit into the mountains with two companions, where he fasted on bread and water; and there he dictated the rule as the Holy Spirit inspired him in his prayer.

(Bonaventure, *Major Life,* IV, II)

43 Foundation of the Third Order

He also founded a Third Order, which is called the Order of Penitents or the Brothers of Penance. Carried away by the force of his preaching, great numbers of people adopted the new rule of penance according to the form instituted by St. Francis which he called the "Order of the Brothers of Penance." The way of penance is common to all those who are on the road to heaven and so this way of life includes members of both sexes, clerics and lay-folk, married or single.

(Bonaventure, *Sermon II* on St. Francis, 1a; and *Major Life,* IV, 6)

Ŝ PAUPTAS·

IN HON. B. P. FRANCISCI SVPRA PRAESEPE ALT. CONSTR.

S·FRA

44 Francis celebrates Christmas in Greccio

45 The Christmas Cave in Greccio

What he did on the birthday of our Lord Jesus Christ near the little town called Greccio in the third year before his glorious death should especially be noted and recalled with reverent memory. In that place there was a certain man by the name of John, and he said to him: "If you want us to celebrate the feast of our Lord at Greccio, go with haste and diligently prepare what I tell you. For I wish to do something that will recall to memory the little Child who was born in Bethlehem and set before our eyes in some way the inconveniences of his infant needs, how he lay in a manger, how, with an ox and an ass standing by, he lay upon the hay where he had been placed." But the day of joy drew near, the time of great rejoicing came and Greccio was made, as it were, a new Bethlehem. The people came and were filled with new joy over the new mystery. The woods rang with the voices of the crowd and the rocks made answer to their jubilation. The saint of God was clothed with the vestments of the deacon, for he was a deacon, and he sang the holy Gospel in a sonorous voice. Then he preached to the people standing about, and he spoke charming words concerning the nativity of the poor King.

(Thomas of Celano, *First Life,* 84-86 (abridged))

46 Vines near Greccio

Once Francis came to a certain place near Bevagna where a very great number of birds of various kinds had congregated, namely, doves, crows, and some others popularly called daws. When the most blessed servant of God, Francis, saw them, being a man of very great fervor and great tenderness toward lower and irrational creatures, he left his companions in the road and ran eagerly toward the birds. When he was close enough to them, seeing that they were waiting expectantly for him, he greeted them in his usual way. But, not a little surprised that the birds did not rise in flight, as they usually do, he was filled with great joy and humbly begged them to listen to the word of God. Among the many things he spoke to them were these words: "My brothers, birds, you should praise your Creator very much and always love him; he gave you feathers to clothe you, wings so that you can fly, and whatever else was necessary for you. God made you noble among his creatures, and he gave you a home in the purity of the air; though you neither sow nor reap, he nevertheless protects and governs you without any solicitude on your part." At these words, as Francis himself used to say and those too who were with him, the birds, rejoicing in a wonderful way according to their nature, began to stretch their necks, extend their wings, open their mouths and gaze at him. And Francis, passing through their midst, went on his way and returned, touching their heads and bodies with his tunic. Finally he blessed them, and then, after he had made the sign of the cross over them, he gave them permission to fly away to some other place. But the blessed father went his way with his companions, rejoicing and giving thanks to God, whom all creatures venerate with humble acknowledgment. But now that he had become simple by grace, not by nature, he began to blame himself for not having preached to the birds before, seeing that they had listened to the word of God with such great reverence. And so it happened that, from that day on, he solicitously admonished all birds, all animals and reptiles, and even creatures that have no feeling, to praise and love their Creator.

(Thomas of Celano, *First Life,* 58)

48 Landscape near Bevagna

Prophet by the Power of the Life of Jesus

49 Francis preaches before Pope Honorius III

Francis was due to preach before the pope and the cardinals on one occasion and at the suggestion of the bishop of Ostia he learned a carefully prepared sermon by heart. But when he stood before them all to deliver his edifying message, his mind went blank and he could not remember a word. He told them what had happened quite humbly and invoked the aid of the Holy Spirit. Then his tongue was suddenly unloosed and he spoke so eloquently that he moved the hearts of his exalted listeners to true sorrow, and it was clear that it was the Spirit of God who spoke, not he.

(Bonaventure, *Major Life*, XII, 7)

50 Landscape near Celano

51 Francis foretells the death of a nobleman of Celano

Another time, after his return from overseas, St. Francis went to preach at Celano and a knight begged him to come and have dinner with him. So he came to the house and the whole family was there to celebrate his arrival with his companions. However, before they sat down St. Francis offered praise to God, as was his custom, and stood there praying, with his eyes raised to heaven. When he had finished, he beckoned his generous host aside and told him, "Brother host, you persuaded me to come and dine with you, and I came. But now do what I tell you immediately, because you are going to eat in another world, not here on this earth. Confess all your sins with genuine sorrow and leave nothing untold. God means to reward you today for having given his poor such a warm welcome." The knight took his advice and confessed all his sins to Francis' companion, and put his affairs in order, doing everything he could to prepare for death. Eventually they took their places at table and just as they were beginning to eat, their host suddenly dropped dead, as the saint had foretold. So it was that as a reward for his kindness in showing hospitality, he received the reward given to prophets, because he had given a prophet the welcome due to a prophet, as we read in the gospel (cf. Mt 10, 41). Warned by the saint's prophecy, the knight had prepared for immediate death and clad in the armor of repentance he escaped eternal damnation and was received into the eternal dwelling-places.

(Bonaventure, *Major Life*, XI, 4)

52 Francis causes water to gush out of a rock for a thirsty man

Another time, while travelling to a hermitage where he planned to devote himself to prayer, St. Francis rode an ass belonging to a poor laborer bcause he felt weak. It was summertime and, as the owner of the animal followed the saint into the mountains, he was exhausted by the long and gruelling journey. Fainting with thirst, he suddenly cried out after the saint. "I'll die of thirst, if I don't get a drink immediately." Francis dismounted there and then and knelt on the ground with his hands stretched out to heaven, and there he prayed until he knew that he had been heard. When he had finished, he told his benefactor, "Go to that rock and you will find running water. Christ in his mercy has made it flow there for you just now." By God's wonderful condescension which responds so easily to his servants, a thirsty human being was able to drink from a rock, quenching his thirst from solid stone, by the power of one man's prayer. Water had never been found at that spot before and none could ever be found there afterwards, although a careful search was made.

(Bonaventure, *Major Life*, VII, 12)

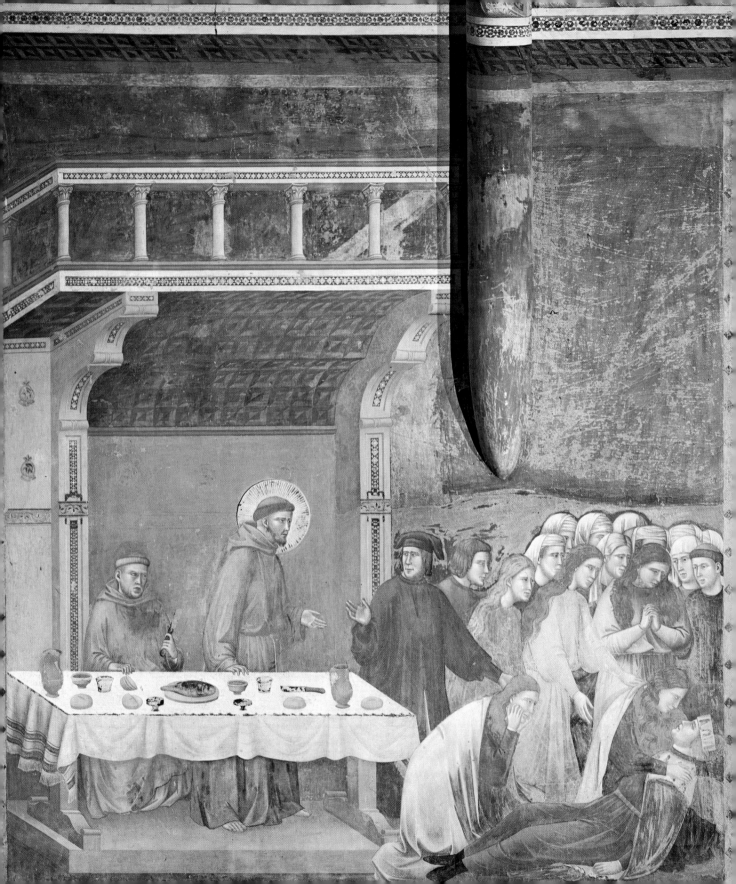

53   Mount La Verna

54   The Cave of Francis on Mount La Verna

55   Francis receives the Stigmata of the Lord

Two years before Francis gave his soul back to heaven, while he was living in the hermitage which was called La Verna, after the place on which it stood, he saw in a vision of God a man standing above him, like a seraph with six wings, his hands extended and his feet joined together and fixed to a cross. Two of the wings were extended above his head, two were extended as if for flight, and two were wrapped around the whole body. When the blessed servant of the Most High saw these things, he was filled with the greatest wonder, but he could not understand what this vision should mean. Still, he was filled with happiness and he rejoiced very greatly because of the kind and gracious look with which he saw himself regarded by the seraph, whose beauty was beyond estimation; but the fact that the seraph was fixed to a cross and the sharpness of his suffering filled Francis with fear. And so he arose sorrowful and joyful, and joy and grief were in him alternately. Solicitously he thought about what this vision could mean, and his soul was in great anxiety to find its meaning. And while he was thus unable to come to any understanding of it and the strangeness of the vision perplexed his heart, the marks of the nails began to appear in his hands and feet, just as he had seen them a little before in the crucified man above him. Furthermore, his right side was as though it had been pierced by a lance and had a wound in it that frequently bled so that his tunic and trousers were very often covered with his blood.

(Thomas of Celano, *First Life,* 94-95)

56   Rocks at the entrance to Francis' cave

57   Francis appears to the brothers at the chapter in Arles

Francis could not preside personally at the chapters of the different provinces, but by his unremitting prayer and the power of his blessing he was always there in spirit in anxious care for his brethren. On one occasion he even appeared visibly at such a chapter by God's power. It was at the chapter of Arles and the famous preacher whom we now honor as St. Anthony was preaching to the friars on the proclamation Pilate wrote on the Cross, "Jesus of Nazareth, the king of the Jews." One of the friars, a holy man named Monaldus, felt a sudden inspiration to look towards the door of the chapter hall; there with his own eyes, he saw St. Francis standing in mid-air with his arms stretched out in the form of a cross, blessing the friars.

(Bonaventure, *Major Life,* IV 10)

58   Clare's little garden at San Damiano where the Canticle of the Sun was composed

59   Christ as Lord of the Universe in the Sun — Mandorla

All praise be yours, my Lord, through all that you have made,
    And first my lord Brother Sun,
    Who brings the day; and light you give to us through him.

(Francis, *Canticle of the Sun*)

Francis sought occasion to love God in everything. He delighted in all the works of God's hands and from the vision of joy on earth his mind soared aloft to the life-giving source and cause of all. In everything beautiful, he saw Him who is beauty itself, and he followed his Beloved everywhere by his likeness imprinted on creation; he made of all creation a ladder by which he might mount up and embrace Him who is all-desirable. He seemed to perceive a divine harmony in the interplay of powers and faculties given by God to his creatures and like the prophet David he exhorted them all to praise God.

(Bonaventure, *Major Life*, IX, 1)

60 Francis rapt in prayer

St. Francis realized that he was an exile from the Lord's presence as long as he was at home in the body (cf. 2 Cor. 5, 6, 8), and his love of Christ had left him with no desire for the things of this earth. Therefore, he tried to keep his spirit always in the presence of God, by praying to him without intermission. He was often taken right out of himself in a rapture of contemplation, so that he was lost in ecstasy and had no idea what was going on about him. Here, too, the friars who were watching heard him cry aloud, imploring God's mercy for sinners, and weeping for the passion of as if he saw it before his eyes. He was occasionally seen raised up from the ground and surrounded with a shining cloud, as he prayed at night with his hands stretched out in the form of a cross. The brilliance which enveloped his body was a sign of the miraculous light which flooded his soul.

(Bonaventure, *Major Life*, X, 1-4 (excerpt))

Death and Transfiguration

61 View of Assisi

For two years after he had received the stigmata — that is twenty years after the beginning of his religious life — Francis endured various illnesses which formed him like a stone ready to be fitted into the heavenly Jerusalem and raised him to the height of perfection, like metal under the blows of a hammer. Then he asked to be brought to St. Mary of the Porziuncola, so that he might yield up his spirit where he had first received the spirit of grace.

(Bonaventure, *Major Life*, XIV, 3)

62 The Death of Francis

When therefore he had rested for a few days in a place he greatly longed to be in and realized that the time of his death was at hand, he called to him two of his brothers and commanded them to sing in a loud voice with joy of spirit the Praises of the Lord over his approaching death, or rather, over the life that was so near. He himself, in as far as he was able, broke forth in that psalm of David: I cried to the Lord with my voice: with my voice I made supplication to the Lord. Francis then commanded that a hair shirt be put upon him and that he be sprinkled with ashes, for he was

soon to become dust and ashes. Then, when many brothers had gathered about, whose father and leader he was, and while they were standing reverently at his side awaiting his blessed death and happy end, his most holy soul was freed from his body and received into the realm of light, and his body fell asleep in the Lord.

(Thomas of Celano, *First Life,* 109-110)

63 Francis' sarcophagus beneath the Lower Church of San Francesco

In 1230 a general chapter of the Order which was attended by a great number of friars was held at Assisi and on May 25 St. Francis' body was transferred to the basilica which had been built in his honor.

(Bonaventure, *Major Life,* XV, 8)

64 Francis appears to Pope Gregory IX in a dream

His Holiness Pope Gregory IX of blessed memory, of whom St. Francis had foretold that he would be pope, was inclined to doubt the wound in Francis' side, before the canonization of the saint. Then one night, as the pope himself used to relate with tears, St. Francis appeared to him in a dream. His face seemed a little stern and he reproached him for his doubts. Then he raised his right arm and showed him the wound and told him to get a glass and catch the blood which was streaming from his side. The pope saw the glass in his vision and it seemed to fill up to the brim with blood.

(Bonaventure, *Major Life,* Part II, I, 2)

65 St. Francis in heavenly glory

While he was there a solemn discussion was held concerning the canonization of the holy man, and the noble assembly of cardinals met often concerning this business. "The most holy life of this most holy man," they said, "needs no attestation of miracles; what we have seen with our eyes, what our hands have handled, we have proved in the light of truth." They immediately appointed the day on which they would fill the whole world with saving happiness. First Pope Gregory preached to all the people, and with a sweet and sonorous voice he spoke of the praise of God. He also praised the holy father Francis in a noble eulogy, and recalling the purity of his life, he was bathed in tears. His sermon had this text: He shone in his days as the morning star in the midst of a cloud, and as the moon at the full. And as the sun when it shines, so did he shine in the temple of God. Then the pope raising his hands to heaven, said: "To the praise and glory of Almighty God and on the advice of our brothers and of the other prelates, we decree that the most blessed father Francis, whom the Lord has glorified in heaven and whom we venerate on earth, shall be enrolled in the catalogue of saints." These things took place in the city of Assisi in the second year of the pontificate of Pope Gregory IX on the sixteenth day of July.

(Thomas of Celano, *First Life,* 123-126 (excerpt))

66 In Rome St. Francis sets free an unjustly imprisoned man

When Gregory IX was pope, a man called Peter, from Alife, was accused of heresy and taken prisoner at Rome, where the pope gave him over to the bishop of Tivoli for safekeeping. The bishop put him in chains, throwing him into a dark dungeon from which there was no escape. There the prisoner was given a ration of food and drink. Then, hearing that it was the vigil of the feast of St. Francis, he entreated him with prayers and tears to have pity on him; he had now purified his faith and renounced all heresy and become a devout follower of St. Francis who was one of Christ's most loyal servants. As a result, he was found worthy to be heard by God, through the merits of St. Francis. At twilight on the evening of his feastday, St. Francis took pity on him and came into his prison. He called him by name and told him to stand up. Peter was terrified and asked who it was. He was told that it was St. Francis. There and then he saw the chains on his feet broken by the power of the saint's presesce. At the same time, some of the iron bolts fell from the stone walls of the cell, so that the walls opened and left the way free for him to escape. He was free but he was so overcome that he could not make his escape; instead he rushed to the door of the cell and frightened the guards with his cries. They told the bishop how he had been freed from his bonds; and when he had heard the whole story, he visited the prison himself. There he realized clearly that the power of God had been at work and he fell down to worship him. The chains were shown to the pope and the cardinals; and when they saw what had happened, they were amazed and gave thanks to God.

(Bonaventure, *Major Life,* Part II, V, 4)

67 Trajan's Column at Rome

68 St. Francis saves a man of Lerida

At Lerida in Catalonia a man called John who was very devoted to St. Francis was walking along a road one evening where an ambush had been laid with intent to kill. John himself had no enemies, but the attack was intended for his companion who bore a close resemblance to him. One of the assailants sprang from his hiding place and, thinking John was his enemy, he attacked him so fiercely with his sword that there was no hope for his recovery. The very first blow he received severed his shoulder and arm almost completely from his body; and another thrust pierced his chest, making such a gash that the escaping breath would have blown out half a dozen candles. The doctors were convinced that he could not be saved; so he had recourse to St. Francis, begging his intercession as fervently as he could. As he lay there alone on his bed of pain, fully conscious and repeating the name Francis continually, a man dressed in the habit of the Friars Minor entered by the window and stood beside him, as it seemed to him. He addressed him by name and said, "You had confidence in me, and so God will save you." When the dying man asked him who he was, he replied that he was St. Francis and immediately bent over him and unwound his bandages. Then he seemed to anoint all his wounds with ointment. The moment John felt the touch of those holy hands which drew their power of healing from our Savior's stigmata, his flesh was renewed and the pus disappeared so that his wounds closed up and he was completely restored to health.

(Bonaventure, *Major Life,* Part II, I, 5)

69 East Doorway and Rose Window of the Upper Church of San Francesco in Assisi

70 View of Assisi

May God bless you, Assisi; for by you many souls will be saved, in you many servants of the Most High will dwell, and out of you many will be chosen for heaven. Peace be with you!

(Francis' farewell blessing on his native city)

71 The Glorification of the Franciscan Order

The Illustrations

1 View of Assisi. The history of the city of Francis, which today numbers about 30,000 inhabitants, reaches back to Roman times, from which are preserved an amphitheatre and the façade of a temple. The town, at an elevation of 424 m., lies at the foot of Mt. Subasio (1290 m. high).

2 View through a lane in Assisi to the "Stalleta," the stable in which Francis is said to have been born between an ox and an ass in 1182. This tradition emphasizes the assimilation of the life of Francis to that of Jesus. The chapel of San Francesco il Piccolo is found here today.

3 Troubadours. Fresco (c.1320) by Simone Martini in St. Martin's Chapel in the Lower Church of San Francesco at Assisi. The young Francis admired the style and way of life of the troubadours. Later he called himself and his companions "God's Troubadours."

4 The "Rocca Maggiore," the fortress above Assisi. In the year 1200, the citizens of Assisi conquered and destroyed this stronghold of the Hohenstaufen emperors and declared the town a republic. The ruins seen today date from the fourteenth century.

5 The townhall at Perugia (1293) makes us recognize the importance of this town which goes back to Etruscan times, and which in Francis' day was at war with Assisi.

6 A man pays homage to the young Francis in the marketplace at Assisi. Fresco (1296 - 1300) by Giotto on the wall on the righthand side of the Upper Church of San Fancesco. Showing the façade of temple of Minerva, which is still standing today. this fresco is one of the earliest examples of Italian art. The picture belongs to a cycle of 28 scenes from the life of Francis, which extends along both sides of the aisle and was partly painted by pupils of Giotto from his sketches. In theme and arrangement the pictures stand in strict iconographic and historical relationship with the scenes from the Old and the New Testament which are depicted higher up.

7 Façade of the Roman temple of Minerva (1st century B.C.) in the marketplace of Assisi. It forms the entrance to the church of Santa Maria sopra Minerva.

8 Road at Collestrada near the bridge of San Giovanni over the Tiber. Here Francis fell into captivity in 1202 when the city militia of the Republic of Assisi suffered a crushing defeat by the troops of the nearby town of Perugia which was still ruled by the nobility.

9 View of the town of Spoleto. Here in 1205 Francis, when he was on his way to the army of the papal general Walter of Brienne, had a vision of the Lord, which led him to abandon life in the world.

13 The cross of San Damiano. Twelfth-century painting on wood in the Byzantine style. Today in the basilica of Santa Chiara in Assisi.

10 Francis gives his cloak to a poor knight. Fresco by Giotto (cf. no. 6).

14 View of the cathedral of San Rufino in Assisi. Francis was baptized in this church, with a beautiful Romanesque façade, begun in 1140. The cathedral is dedicated to the martyr-bishop Rufino (+239), who brought Christianity to Assisi.

11 View of San Damiano. Here in 1206 Francis, when he was praying in the church threatened with decay, had a decisive encounter with Christ who appealed to him from the painted crucifix to rebuild his house.

15 Francis cuts himself off from his father. Fresco by Benozzo Gozzoli (1420-1497) in the church of San Francesco in Montefalco (now a museum). Because of its splendid situation, the town is called the "Umbrian Balcony." The event took place in front of the Bishop's Palace at Assisi, near San Rufino (cf. no. 14) in the year 1206 (ca.).

12 Francis prays before the cross in San Damiano. Fresco by Giotto (cf. no. 6).

16 Ruins of a Romanesque chapel near Spello. The chapel of the Porziuncola and the other churches that Francis restored after his experience in San Damiano must have looked like this.

17 The chapel of Santa Maria degli Angeli, called the Porziuncola, belonged originally to the Benedictine monastery on Monte Subasio. Francis felt himself drawn to this lonely place. In 1207 he restored the church and on February 24, 1209, he recognized his calling in the Gospel read here. Today there stands above the Porziuncola, the centre of the Franciscan world, the Basilica of Santa Maria degli Angeli, a baroque basilica with three naves, which was built according to the plans of the architect G. Alessi of Perugia between 1569 and 1679 (about 4 km. from Assisi).

18 Francis cares for a cripple. Detail from the Francis-panel by Bonaventura Berlinghieri (1235-1274) in the church of San Francesco at Pescia. The panel is numbered among the earliest representations of Francis and his life.

19 Franciscans preaching. Panel by B. Berlinghieri (cf. no. 18).

20 Belfry of the small, Romanesque church of San Stefano in Assisi built in 1166. According to legend, the single bell is said to have sounded at the moment of Francis' death, without anyone having pulled the bell-rope.

21 View of the town of Trevi. Francis went past this place on his way to Rome in 1209 with his first twelve companions. The lay-out on the mountain is typical of Umbrian towns, often built on the site of former Etruscan settlements.

22 Dream of Pope Innocent III, who sees a man (Francis) supporting the great papal church of St. John Lateran. Fresco by B. Gozzoli (cf. no. 15).

23 After his dream, in which he recognizes the significance of Francis and his young company, Pope Innocent III blesses the champion of poverty and confirms his Rule and his new order. The fresco, by B. Gozzoli (cf. no. 15), shows Pope Honorius III granting his approval of the final Rule by a bull of November 29, 1223 (cf. no. 36).

24 Lane in Assisi with houses of Francis' day.

25 St. Clare. Fresco by Simone Martini (1284-1344) in the right transept of the Lower Church of San Francesco. Clare, born in Assisi in 1194 the daughter of the nobleman, Favarone di Offreduccio, became the mother of the "Poor Ladies," the Second Order, which Francis founded.

29 Tower of the basilica of Santa Chiara at Assisi. The church erected 1257-1260 on the site of the old church of San Giorgio (where the body of Francis lay until its translation to San Francesco), with the adjoining convent, has been since 1260 the centre of the order of St. Clare, whose remains rest in the crypt.

26 The induction of Clare. Detail of a Clare-panel (cf. no. 28). After her flight from the home of her parents who opposed her vocation to the religious life, she was clothed as the first Poor Clare by Francis in the chapel of the Porziuncola.

30 Francis establishes peace in Arezzo (1217), where through Brother Silvester he drove out the devil who had stirred up civil war. Fresco by Giotto (cf. no. 6).

27 Refectory in San Damiano. From 1212 to 1260, San Damiano was the mother house of the order of the Poor Clares. In the vaulted dining-hall, in which Pope Gregory IX was a guest of the Poor Clares in 1228, a bunch of flowers marks St. Clare's place to this day.

31 View of Arezzo. In the center is the five-story tower (1330) of the twelfth-century church of Pieve di S. Maria with a three-story façade of arcades.

28 Panel of St. Clare, begun in 1283, ascribed to the Florentine painter, Cimabue (flourished 1272-1302). Today it is in the transept of the church of Santa Chiara at Assisi. The scenes from the lives of the saint depict (from bottom left to bottom right): Clare receiving the palm branch from the bishop of Assisi — Flight to Francis — Clothing in the Porziuncola — Clare clinging to the altar and defying her relations — Clare helping her sister Agnes in her flight to the cloister — The life of poverty in San Damiano — Appearance of our Lady at Clare's death-bed (1253) — Burial of the saint by Pope Innocent IV.

32 Francis and Dominic. Fresco by B. Gozzoli (cf. no. 15). The meeting between the founders of the two orders probably took place in 1215 during the Lateran Council.

33 Isola Maggiore on Lake Trasimene. According to tradition Francis spent forty days of fast on this island before the festival of Easter in 1219.

37 Portrait of Francis. Fresco by Cimabue (c. 1278) in the right transept of the Lower Church of San Francesco in Assisi.

34 View of the hermitage of Le Carceri in the oak-forest of Monte Subasio. Francis sought out the solitude of similar places again and again, when after his preaching-journeys he wanted "to set his thoughts right with God." The present lay-out took shape in the fifteenth century during the extension of the old oratory of our Lady belonging to the Benedictines of Monte Subasio under St. Bernardin of Siena.

38 Harbor at Ancona. In 1219 Francis set out from here on his missionary journey to Egypt and the Holy Land which had just been conquered by the knights of the fifth crusade. The painting in this montage, from the Uffizi Gallery in Florence, depicts a miracle of St. Francis who saved a boat from being swamped.

35 Cave of Brother Matteo near the hermitage of Le Carceri. In such caves, formed in the rock, Francis and his brothers lived as hermits in strict poverty.

39 Francis demonstrates before the sultan of Egypt the power of his faith, when he challenges the Muslim holy men in vain to an ordeal by fire. Fresco by Giotto (cf. no6).

36 Bull of Pope Honorius III, by which in 1223 the Rule of the Franciscan Order was confirmed. Assisi, Treasury of San Francesco.

40 Francis is betrothed to Poverty. Fresco (c. 1320) in the vault above the high altar in the Lower Church of San Francesco in Assisi. The artist is considered to have been a disciple of Giotto and is called "Maestro delle Vele."

41 Landscape near Poggio Bustone with a view of the valley of Rieti.

45 The cave of Greccio on the slope of the Sabine mountains, where Francis established the tradition of the Christmas Crib.

42 Cave of Francis near the friary of Fonte Colombo near Rieti, where the founder of the Order set down in writing the second, definitive form of his Rule in 1223.

46 Vines in the neighborhood of the Franciscan shrine at Greccio.

43 This panel, by B. Berlinghieri (cf. no. 18), depicts a healing scene. The man in the middle is a leper with his castanet to warn people of his approach.

47 Francis preaches to the birds. Fresco (c. 1236) on the side-wall of the Lower Church of San Francesco at Assisi. This and other pictures of Francis in the aisle of the Lower Church are ascribed to a painter of the circle of Giunta Pisano called "Maestro di San Francesco" (c. 1202-1255).

44 Francis celebrates Christmas in 1223 at Greccio where he sets up a crib for the first time. Fresco by Giotto (cf. no. 6).

48 Umbrian Landscape near Bevagna. According to tradition it is in this region that Francis is said to have preached to the birds.

49 Francis preaches before Pope Honorius II. Fresco by Giotto (cf. no. 6). This scene possibly depicts the encounter of 1220 when Francis asked the pope to appoint Cardinal Hugolino (later Pope Gregory IX) protector of the Order.

53 Mount La Verna, where Francis received the Stigmata in 1224. The mountain had been given to the saint as early as 1213 by Count Orlando di Chiusi, and it was much valued by Francis for its lonely situation as a place for contemplation and prayer. Today there is to be found on the mountain a spacious friary begun in the fifteenth century.

50 Landscape near Celano. The native city of Thomas of Celano (ca. 1190 - ca. 1260), first biographer of Francis. The fortress overlooking the city was built in the fifteenth century.

54 Cave with the iron-grid that Francis used for a bed on Mount La Verna.

51 Francis warns a nobleman of Celano that he would die shortly. Fresco by Giotto (cf. no. 6).

55 Francis receives the Stigmata of our Lord (on September 17, 1224). Fresco (c.1320) by Pietro Lorenzetti on the front wall of the left transept of the Lower Church of San Francesco at Assisi.

52 Francis causes a spring to gush out of the rock for a man who was accompanying him and had a great thirst. Fresco by Giotto (cf. no. 6).

56 Rock-formation at the entrance to the cave with Francis' bed on Mount La Verna.

57 Francis appears to his brothers at the provincial chapter at Arles during a sermon preached by St. Anthony of Padua. Fresco by Giotto (cf. no. 6).

58 Clare's little garden in the monastery of San Damiano. Here in 1225 originated Francis' "Canticle of the Sun" which the saint, when seriously ill, composed as a hymn of praise to God and his creation.

59 Christ, as Lord of the Universe, enthroned in the Sun — Mandorla. Relief (twelfth century) on the façade of the cathedral of San Rufino in Assisi.

60 Francis is watched by his brothers to see how, rapt in prayer, he is raised above the ground. This fresco by Giotto (cf. no. 6) depicts Christ's answer to Francis: "Nothing in this Rule is yours; for, all is Mine" (cf. *Omnibus of Sources*, p. 1125).

61 View of Assisi. From this spot Francis blessed his hometown when on October 1, 1226, he was taken dying from the Bishop's Palace to the Porziuncola.

62 The death of Francis. Fresco on the wall of the aisle in the Lower Church of San Francesco at Assisi (cf. no. 47).

63 Francis' sarcophagus in the crypt under the Lower Church of San Francesco. The mortal remains of the saint were placed under the main altar of the Lower Church of San Francesco on May 25. 1230. The sarcophagus was first exposed in 1818 and placed in the crypt in 1824. It acquired its present form in 1932.

64 Francis appears to the sleeping Pope Gregory IX and convinces him of the genuinenes of his Stigmata. Fresco by Giotto (cf. no. 6). This miracle must have taken place shortly before the canonization which the pope proclaimed on July 16, 1228.

65 St. Francis in heavenly glory. Fresco in the vault above the high altar of the Lower Church of San Francesco at Assisi (cf. no. 40).

66 In Rome St. Francis sets free Peter of Alife, imprisoned unjustly for heresy. Fresco by Giotto (cf. no. 6). Also in this picture as in picture no. 6 the artist has given a clear indication of the place of the occurrence by the representation of Trajan's Column.

67 Trajan's Column in Trajan's Forum in Rome. Erected in A.D. 113, the column, 29m. high, bears scenes in relief depicting Caesar's victorious war against the Dacians.

68 St. Francis heals a deadly wound of a man of the town of Lerida in Spain, who had a special devotion to him.

69 East doorway and rose window of the Upper Church of San Francesco at Assisi. The building of the church enshrining the tomb of Francis was begun immediately after the death of the saint. The Lower Church very likely was finished by 1230. The Upper Church, one of the finest buildings of Italian Gothic, was consecrated in 1253.

70 View of Assisi. To the left the grounds of the church and friary of San Francesco. The "Sacro Convento" with its huge buttresses attained its present form under Pope Sixtus IV (1471-1481).

71 The glorification of Francis and his Order. Flemish Gobelin, given in 1479 by Pope Sixtus IV to the friary of San Francesco in Assisi, today on the front wall of the papal hall of the Sacro Convento. The representation arranged after the pattern of a tree of life (*Arbor Franciscana*) displays prominent personalities who have come from the Order of St. Francis (among others, three popes, St. Elizabeth of Thuringia of Hungary, St. Anthony of Padua, St. Bonaventure, St. Clare).